CONTENTS

EAT LIKE A LOCAL	9
Me and Pho and a Dog called Phu	13
Where In The World Did Those Two Expats Go?	15
Insider Tips To Get The Best Out Of Vietnam	17
There Are Three Ways To Eat Street Food	19
Vietnamese Street Food. A Very Brief History	23
Seasonal Street Food Snacks	25
The Famous Pho Soup	26
Choosing A Place To Eat	27
Street Food Or Restaurants	29
YOUR CULINARY COMPASS FOR VIETNAM	31
THE NORTH	33
Miền Luồn	35
Eel vermicilli	35
Lu'o'n Nu'o'ng Xa	37
Eel chargrilled with lemongrass	37
Lươn Om Nước Sốt	38
Eel braised with caramel sauce	38
Bún Thang	40
Chicken noodle soup	40
Bún Thang Hà Nội	40
Bún Bò Nam Bộ	42
Southern beef noodle soup	42
Bún Bò	43
Beef soup	43
Bún Với Rau Thơm	45
Vermicelli salad	45
Bò Mật Ong Khòi	46
Honey-cured beef	46

Nước Cham	47
Dipping sauce	47
Đậu Phộng Rang	48
Roasted peanuts	48
Hẹ Tây Chiên	49
Fried red Asian shallots	49
Bún Bò Hue	50
Beef noodle soup from Hue	50
Bánh Cuốn	50
Fresh rice rolls	50
Bánh Cuốn Nông	52
Steamed ravioli rolls	52
Nước Mắm	55
Fish sauce dip	55
Bún Chả	56
Pork barbecued patties	56
Bún Chả	57
Barbeque pork patties	57
Mỳ Gà Tần	59
Chicken soup	59
Bún Mộc	60
Meatballs and noodle soup	60
Bún Mộc Hà Nội	61
Hanoi pork balls and vermicelli soup	61
Bánh Ghoi	63
Pillow-shaped pastry	63
Chao	64
Rice gruel	64
Cháo Gao	64
Clam gruel	64
Bánh Đúc	65
Spicy gruel	65
Cháo Ga	66
Chicken gruel	66
Muc Nương	67
Barbecued dried squid	67
Bun Rieu Cua	68
Crab soup	68
Bun Rieu	69
Crab noodle soup	69
Bun Oc	70
Snail soup	70

VIETNAM'S REGIONAL STREET FOODIES GUIDE

FIFTY OF THE BEST STREET FOODS IN VIETNAM AND WHERE TO EAT THEM

INCLUDES FAMOUS STREET FOOD RECIPES TO COOK BACK HOME

PAGE ADDIE PRESS
UNITED KINGDOM. AUSTRALIA

Copyright©2016 Fat Noodle Books
All rights reserved. No reproduction, copy or transmission of this
Publication may be made without written permission from the author.
No paragraph of this publication may be reproduced, copied or transmitted
Save with written permission or in accordance with provisions of the Copyright,
Designs and Patents Act 1988, or under the terms of any license permitting limited
copying, issued by the Copyright Licensing Agency,
The Author has asserted his right to be identified as the author
Of this work in accordance with the Copyright, Design and Patents Act 1988
Vietnam's Regional Street Foodies Guide. The Best Fifty Street Foods in Vietnam And
Where To Eat Them. ISBN 978-0-9946350-3-7
BIC Subject category: 1 Travel-Vietnam. 2 Cooking-Vietnamese. 3 Food- Vietnamese.
4 Translations-Vietnamese to English. 5 Travel Guidebook. 6 Street food-Vietnamese.
Published in Australia by Page Addie.
An imprint of Page Addie Press Great Britain.
A catalogue record for this book is available from the Australian Library.

Nem	71
Spring roll	71
Xôi Xéo	72
Sticky rice	72
Xôi Xéo	74
Sticky rice	74
Peanut and Sesame Dip	75
Pho Bo	75
Beef soup	75
Pho Bo	77
Rice noodle soup with beef	77
Quick Pho	80
Bánh Đa Trộn	81
Bún Dọc Mùng	82
Pork and noodle soup	82
Bánh Tôm	82
Prawn dumplings	82
Bánh Xèo Hanoi Style	83

SNACKS — 85

Hoa Quả Dầm	85
Fruit in a glass	85
Chè Đậu Đen	86
Sweet black bean drink	86
Xoi Chè	86
Sticky rice topped with sweetened mung bean paste.	86
Chè Thập Cẩm	87
Chè Khúc Bạch	88
Rainbow drink	88
Chè Chuối	89
Banana in coconut milk	89
Cà Phê Trung	91
Egg coffee	91

Hanoi-Barbecue — 92

Best Duck — 93

Best Skewers — 93

CENTRAL VIETNAM — 95

Cao Lầu	95
Noodles and pork hot pot	95

Bánh	96
Steamed rice buns	96
Bánh Khọt	97
Hollow cake	97
Cơm Hến	98
Rice and seafood	98
Mì Quảng	98
Bún Thịt Nướng	99
Bun Bo Hue	100
Banh Khoai	100
Savory pancake	100
Banh Xeo Chay	101
Rice flour crepe	101
Banh Xeo Tom	103
Crepe with prawn and enoki mushroom filling	103
Bun Cha Ca	105
Fish cakes and rice noodles	105

THE SOUTH 107

Xôi Bui Thi Xuan	107
Savory or sweet glutinous rice	107
Cao Lầu Saigon	108
Bánh Xèo Saigon	108
Savory pancakes	108
Bún Đậu Mắm Tôm	109
Shrimp tofu	109
Đậu Phụ Sốt Cà Chua	110
Fried tofu in tomato sauce	110
Tau Hu Xa Ot	111
Lemongrass crusted tofu	111
Bún Bò Hue	112
Beef noodle soup	112
Bánh Mì	113
Bread roll	113
Canh Bún	113
Phở Bò	114
Beef soup	114
Mỳ Quảng	114
Cơm Hến	115
Bún Mọc	116
Gỏi Cuốn / Bì Cuốn	116
Freshly wrapped spring rolls	116
Bun Thit Nuong	117
Cháo	118

Cơm Tấm	118
Broken rice and shredded pork	118
Bún Mắm	119
Bánh Tầm Bì	120
Hand made noodles	120
Bánh Canh Trảng Bàng	120
Bánh Khọt	121
Canh Bún	122
Crab soup	122
Bột Chiên	122
Best Tabletop Grills	123
Best Poultry	123
Skewers in Ho Chi Minh	124
Sauces	125

EAT LIKE A LOCAL

Want to know where the best street food is in Vietnam? Look no further! Take it from us, two self-confessed street foodies. If anyone can show you the street foods of Vietnam, we can.

We came to Vietnam for a six week vacation, and ended up spending eight years here. Over the last eight years, we've put together the most popular and famous street food dishes in Vietnam, and the places we've discovered which we return to again and again.

Vietnam has over 600 street food dishes but when you're travelling, you don't have time to try every dish. That's why, in this volume, we have selected only the most famous and most loved street foods. An essential foodies guide to the Vietnamese dishes most popular with the locals, North, Central and South.

You may, like us, arrive after a long haul flight and immediately wonder what this noisy and busy place called Vietnam is all about. In fact, the hustle and bustle might make you head to the nearest western style cafe and order a buffalo burger, just to get off the street for a moment! But we'll let you into our secret: the Vietnamese culture is held in a bowl of fragrant jasmine tea and a steaming pot of Pho. It's not until the moment you order street food, that your true Vietnamese experience starts. Here's the reason why: eating with locals and eating like a local, is the quickest way to get to the heart of the Vietnamese people and their country. By experiencing authentic street food, you truly discover the Vietnam the locals know, her quiet, serene, spiritual, peaceful side, her warm heart. Even if your Vietnamese travel days have a limited time frame of a week, you can leave knowing you have tried the most popular street food dishes Vietnam has to offer.

So let two expatriates take you down the alleys and side streets of Vietnam. In this book, the third in the Fat Noodle Books Vietnam travel series, you'll discover which regional Vietnamese street food dishes are at the culinary heart and soul of Vietnam. The best fifty Vietnamese food your dong will buy.

Be prepared to save money, at around $2 a meal, street food takes your travel dollars further. Be prepared to eat too, but you won't need to loosen your belt to do it! Most street food dishes get a heart tick for fresh ingredients and veritable cornucopia of local fruit and vegetables.

Recipes our Vietnamese friends and local vendors kindly shared with us, are included for this regional street food edition.

This means you can 'Eat Like a Local ®' on holiday and when you get back home, cook the same delicious dishes in your own kitchen.

The ingredients are readily found in Asian food stores and no special kitchen utensils are needed. If you can't find an ingredient, don't sweat it; simply substitute with another related ingredient, e.g. fresh or packet noodles, thin or flat. Vary the ingredients. That way, you are cooking like the locals do: following traditional regional recipes and using fresh, seasonal produce.

Traditional recipes vary, depending on the dish, the local ingredients, cooking methods, as do the tasty accompaniments. Treasured Vietnamese family recipes are often kept secret and handed down through generations. While few of the 600 street food specialties are known outside the country, there are dishes that are legends around the world. You can eat pho served up by Phuong's mother in Da Tuong Street in the French Quarter of Hanoi (known as the Paris of the East) for $2. Or you can eat pho, in a restaurant in Paris or Sydney, for $$$$. The same ingredients: rice noodles, a steaming beef broth with a hint of star anise and black pepper, fresh spring onions floating on top and slices of beef.

Wherever you are in the world, one dish or another transports you back in memory to another place and time. That is the quality of authentic delicious foods. The taste experience stays with you. This fact is why pho, a hearty Vietnamese beef noodle soup, is one of the most famous street food dishes in Vietnam and has taken up celebrity status in the culinary world.

Me and Pho and a Dog called Phu

We have our own story about Pho (famouse Vietnamese soup). In Da Tuong Street, we lived with our rescue dog Phu, a dog native to Phu Quoc Island seen in the photograph here. The moment we brought Phu home, sitting calmly between us on the back of our motorbike during rush hour traffic, Phu was family. She was a great dog but had a mind of her own and a long 18 month puppyhood of getting up to mischief. We nicknamed her 'Chewy' on account of her episodes chewing electric cords (only the ones not plugged into a socket) shoes, computer cords and even an enormous hole in the middle of a mattress. She liked to eat. On leash for walks, Phu was always on the lookout for food, the ancestor altars set up outside restaurants with food offerings to bring luck and fortune, fair game. Despite Phu's expensive diet of western quality dog biscuits, she was a beach style scavenger in the city, part of her breed, her survivalist nature. It took a while, but after months of dog training by the book, we taught her to 'come', 'sit' and 'eat' from her own doggy bowl. She appeared to outgrow her extended puppyhood and behave like a well-trained dog should. We thought.

One morning, we all took our constitutional walk along the street, with Phu walking along obediently at the end of her new pink suede leash. When we got back to our apartment, we were horrified to see Phu's theft hanging from her jowls. She'd grabbed a large roll of beef, right off a street vendor's table and walked back with it between her teeth without us even noticing. The dear lady on the stall in the alley had tied tender beef with string and simmered the roll in a spicy broth. She'd set the beef on the cutting board, ready to be sliced for pho soup to make her living feeding the regulars who'd stop at her stall for breakfast, on their way to work. But this cold winter morning, her beef roll was missing and we had one guilty dog. We took the meat back to the vendor and made our apologies on behalf of Phu. The woman was not pleased. She initially refused compensation, but eventually she took the money. We turned her into a millionaire for the morning. She pocketed the million VND and closed the stall early that day.

After that, we'd walk past the stall with Phu on a new short leash, because we knew Phu was always going to have her beef, if she could get half a chance.

Where In The World Did Those Two Expats Go?

Eventually, the generosity of the continual government visas came to an end, a British novelist took over our rental lease, bought our motorbike and houselot of furniture we had accumulated. We rehoused Phu with a Canadian couple. We also left behind wonderful expat friends and long-time Vietnamese friends.

On the day we finally left Hanoi for good, a local woman, Huong, on seeing our bags said 'But why are you leaving, you are so happy here!' She made us smile. We accepted the fact that we had simply fallen in love with the place, and we continue to come back here to what we consider to be our second home with our extended Vietnamese family.

Another Vietnamese friend let us into a secret, when we said goodbye, Dinh said, "Vietnamese don't like to say goodbye, because goodbye means forever. So please just say 'See you later'. Don't tell us sad truths, never say you are leaving."

That was how we left it. As far as the locals are concerned we are on holiday. We will come back, and we do. It surprises us how many times we stopover in Vietnam. Our dear friend, Poet Mai Van Phan says, 'You have the Red River running through your veins now.' And perhaps he is right.

Whenever we stopover in Vietnam, we return to our favorite places, to have tea, coffee and to eat on the street. We feel like we return to our big Vietnamese family. Nothing much changes, except additions like an extra baby or two. As soon as they see us, a broad genuine smile happens, locals never forget a face; we are greeted like long lost family members. Some think we still live there!

We've eaten on the streets of Da Nang, Hue, Hoi An, Nha Trang, Ho Chi Minh and Hanoi. It is extraordinary how the food and cooking styles have stayed in our memories; a bowl of spicy beef noodle soup, Saigon style, the fragrance of mint, chili and lemongrass... transports us right back to the streets of Saigon, a bowl of steaming broth, smiling faces, a winter's morning.

Insider Tips To Get The Best Out Of Vietnam

Talk to any expats or tourist and most everyone agrees, Vietnam cities are comparatively demanding environments. So how can you cope and not let the excessive demands dominate your travel? Take our experience as a shortcut to enjoying your days, weeks and months travelling in Vietnam. Try these five expat rules: avoid getting overtired (think about taking an afternoon nap, like a local); avoid getting overheated (wear only breathable fabrics, no silk clothing or technical clothing); wear light cottons and the thinnest linen in the heat of summer and don't overdress (less is more comfortable); drink plenty of fluids, eat and drink for the season (lime and water with a pinch of salt and some sugar makes an electrolyte drink the locals swear by); save your personal energy (catch a cab to get from A to B on long stretches of busy streets e.g don't attempt to walk down paint and pipe street, to get to the Temple of Literature) and when crossing the road remember the locals don't have as much respect for a zebra crossings or red lights as you do. Be decisive when crossing a road in traffic, keep an eye on the traffic as you walk, don't run (never chicken out and step backwards, but go forth with intent) and you might just get to the other side of the road! The final and most important tip to enjoying Vietnam is this. Take advantage of the difference, keep up the humor and have fun. Oh, we almost forgot...bring industrial quality foam earplugs to ensure a good nights sleep, wherever you are. There is always a rooster crowing or a dog barking or a motorbike horn tooting someplace!

There Are Three Ways To Eat Street Food

Street food has always been described as food for the common people, mostly laborers. Defined as cheap eats, readily available, sold and eaten in alleys or carried around by street hawkers. You can buy 'hang rong' meaning food that is carried around for sale, from basket women, the icons of street food sellers who balance two baskets laden with food between a wooden yoke across their shoulders, or carry food in baskets balanced on the top of their heads. Some walk for kilometers into the city center. They stop along the street in the same place at the same time of day. They set up temporarily, if they have not paid street tax to set up cooking, they always have an eye out for local police who fine them and/or confiscate their baskets and food. If the basket woman suddenly packs up and runs off, you know why. It's not you!

The second way to eat street food is to buy from women

who set up temporary venues outside or near their homes, on the sidewalk, alleys or outside cafes at certain times of the day.

During our time in Vietnam we made a point of supporting street food culture, just like the locals do. Vietnamese locals frequent the same individual street and small food stands everyday. Vietnamese prefer to eat street food where food is prepared and cooked fresh in front of them. Ask any local why they eat on the street and they'll tell you, the food is so much tastier than in a restaurant. In the time it takes to dunk rice noodles into a fragrant broth, you can eat like a local, sitting as they do on small red or blue plastic chairs, watching and waiting while a street cook, prepares the food to her recipe.

The third way to eat street food is at established street food venues that have been serving traditional recipes for generations. The history behind bricks and mortar venues comes from the 1800's, when the idea of sitting down outside was for unskilled or low-skilled laborers. Women in particular, would never eat on the street. Instead women would go inside the cook's house to eat, rather than sit outside.

Today, the families of the same vendors are still serving up treasured family recipes; you'll come across crowded and popular street restaurants: tables set up inside and on the pavement outside. Inside there are wash hand basins; food is cooked in stainless steel pans; ingredients stored in fridges and precooked food is presented in glass cabinets; cooking is either done on a barbeque using compressed fuel bricks or on a gas burner cooktop. You can watch the woman cooking your food, and while you sit at a plastic table, on a plastic chair you can't help feeling like you are someone's living room, the family alter with its fresh flowers and burning incense, (note the locals prefer you not to look and not to photograph) TV on a local channel and yes, sometimes, a food and trading certificate, hanging in pride of place, on the wall. Yes, often it is their living room. Whatever the décor, don't be put off if the limewashed walls look desperately in need of a lick of paint and the French mosaic floor tiles look unscrubbed and well-trodden. You are lucky enough to be in a place, where time has stood still and you are looking at history that is fast disappearing. The locals seem bent on pulling down French colonial buildings and the ones we asked indicated they wanted a modern city, more like Singapore or South Korea. So enjoy the now and the colonial era vibe that goes along with it.

Vietnamese Street Food. A Very Brief History

Charles-Eduard Hocquard, a French doctor and photographer, cited street stalls in his book *Thirty Months in Tonkin*. His book contains photographs of the food stalls along the Hanoi to Bac Ninh road in the 1920's during the French occupation. The French built roads and streets in Hanoi, Saigon and other major cities enabling people to leave the countryside and settle in cities. To cater for the increasing urban population, street food stalls opened, serving unique regional foods. With the advent of electricity, street stalls opened in the evenings.

In the 1920's, Thach Lam, a food writer wrote: "There is no time in a day that one can't find street food. Each hour is a different time; eating street food is an art: one has to eat at the right hour and buy it from that right person - that's how to become a connoisseur of the food." We think the same is true of street food today. Really, only the way people serve it has changed. Take xoi lua, (sticky rice with mung bean paste) once women carried it in baskets, but today, xoi lua is served in street food stalls, with additions to the original recipe like sausages, pork, chicken and eggs. Another example of the evolution of street food is bun bo, noodle soup with beef. Once upon a time, Hue vendors prepared this dish in An Cuu village and then walked kilometers to Hue City to sell it. Today, vendors ride motorbikes over Trang Tien Bridge to sell their bun bo specialty in the markets.

Vietnam food styles are changing rapidly, as are the cities themselves. Take the Old Quarter of Hanoi. Plans are well underway to move the local families out of the Old Quarter to high rise buildings in the countryside. The valuable land, that has housed the same generations of families, once vacated, will be turned into a banking and financial district with office blocks. Now is the time to *carpe diem* and seize the moment of every travel day to eat like a local and discover street food, before restaurants take over and street food as you find it today, becomes a distant memory of the past. Just in case!

Seasonal Street Food Snacks

In Vietnamese, 'an qua' translates to 'eating snacks'. We think of it as seasonal eating. In winter, you find street vendors deep frying slices of taro, potato, pumpkin and bananas. Winter warmers served hot from the frying pan and wrapped in newspaper. In hot summer months keep an eye out for che drinks with crushed ice, taro, tapioca and fruit, yogurt drinks, sugar cane juice, and don't miss a refreshing drink served with black jelly squares (for cooling the body) with crushed ice, coconut milk and topped with shredded coconut. In Autumn, vendors sell steamed young green rice, a seasonal specialty, wrapped in a lotus leaf parcel, delicious eaten back at the hotel room, along with an accompanying bite of sweet green banana.

The Famous Pho Soup

What's in a soup? Pho has made it from the streets of Vietnam to the restaurants of Paris. Huge accolades for a simple dish. When meeting a Vietnamese local, one of the first thing they ask, practicing their English, is this question: "Do you like Pho?" (pronounced 'Fur' in Vietnamese). It's a national dish that begs the question. One dish you have to try so you can give them an honest answer.

We often say "Khong" (no) practicing our Vietnamese, they look shocked and say "khong hieu?" meaning I don't understand why you don't love Pho as much as we do, (kind of extended translation). Don't get us wrong; we have eaten the most delicious pho, such soup is made with love, you can taste it: if the soup has been made using a traditional recipe, soup bones simmered on an open fire overnight. That's makes for tasty pho. Unfortunately we have also had insipid tasting pho. Why the difference? Well it's fantastic when the stock has been made from a traditional recipe, but bad when the recipe is made from a packet of stock, a packet of salt and a bagful of M.S.G for seasoning. It's not a no no to eat pho, more of a heads up to the changing times of less simmering meat cuts and more shortcuts to make the broth base. We ate many a bowl of pho, which is why we have addresses in this book of places that serve only the most excellent of pho. We figure life is too short to eat anything less than best.

Choosing A Place To Eat

Eat where the crowds eat. Good street food places remain popular because the vendor cares about the food and the place has a good food vibe. Eat at places that are busy. That is a street foodie rule. The more customers, the higher the turnover and the fresher the food will be.

Eat at one-dish specialty vendor stalls, because it signals a seller who buys that day and then cooks fresh food until it runs out. That way you can eat food that has just been prepared and hasn't been left sitting around.

Lunchtime is at 11am; eat when the Vietnamese do, at a first sitting. Observe how the locals eat and copy them, if you aren't sure. Locals are your best culinary guides. If they add garlic or herbs, or order a double helping of squid, do as they do. They will know how fresh the food is and what flavors marry up. If they add chili or pick vermicelli noodles over thick ones, do what the locals do.

We avoid communal chopsticks like the plague because wood is a germ-fest, no matter how pretty with inlaid mother-of-pearl they are. You see people wiping down chopsticks and spoons with paper napkins or wet wipes to remove germs. While it looks like it could be affective, the technique is totally useless. Instead wipe down the chopsticks with natural antiseptics such as lime and chili condiments on the table. Better still, bring your own disposable chopsticks, on sale in markets and supermarkets. When you sit down to eat, order hot tea, then use hot tea to rinse out cups and rinse off bowls, the way the locals do. If it feels weird, don't worry. It is expected! Simply pour a small amount of tea, swill the hot tea around and tip the tea out on the ground, then pour a cup to drink.

Street Food Or Restaurants

While restaurants serve street food style dishes, authentic street is still the choice of the locals. The slice of daily life on the street and social interaction is a key ingredient. By comparison, the air-conditioned restaurants of Hanoi and Saigon have many dishes on the menu. To cater economically, they often make one stockpot, for two or more different recipes. One broth for all dishes. The taste of one recipe is not distinct from the other. That is why you can eat a meal consisting of many dishes and feel like you have eaten the same thing. But the street vendor knows to make the base stock special, using their own traditional recipe handed down through generations, to use ingredients like star anise and cinnamon, and to let the soup bones simmer in the pot on the fire overnight until morning. If you are lucky enough to find a local place, the food you eat will be part of your culinary memory, for sure.

If you eat in tourist restaurants or hotels, from our experience, expect to be served an east/west tourist fusion style of food. Expensive and often not value for money. The worst being meals organized by tour operators where the food tastes like food from an Asian food hall. Or worse, you are eating in a food hall place with mass produced M.S.G laden greasy spoon food. So, if you are a foodie, take control of the meal part of your itinerary and avoid leaving it up to tour operators who will take you to where they think foreigners want to eat! Even if they say otherwise.

We always said, we would leave Hanoi when the fires on the streets go out. Sadly, we have seen less street food and more restaurants serving bland street food on the menu. We have been to restaurants where 'imitation street food vendors' set up in a courtyard, dressed in traditional clothes dishing up foods on white china, where the credit card takes precedence. It lacks the uniquely Vietnamese phenomenon that is such a part of the Vietnamese day.

YOUR CULINARY COMPASS FOR VIETNAM

THE NORTH

In Northern recipes, fresh ginger, spring onions, red and green chili, fish sauce, basil, mint, Thai holy basil, coriander and traditional herbs like perilla leaves are added in generous proportions to the dishes. The garlic is particularly sweet, mild and nutty. Phu Quoc Island black pepper, which is intensely aromatic, give street food it's distinctive Northern taste.

The local villages specialize in making signature fresh bun (noodles) and the thin rice wrappers used for making spring rolls. A culinary art with recipes handed down through generations.

Rice is a staple at the table. There is a saying, in the North, the Vietnamese grow rice crops four times a year; in the South they watch the rice grow and in neighboring Laos, they listen to it grow. So the Vietnamese are good with rice.

Northern Vietnam is proud of their short grain rice, grown locally and served steamed or fried. A bowl of steamed rice is central to the Vietnamese meal, spooned into the bowl and refilled often during the course of the meal. Add condiments and whatever smaller side dishes are available on the table. Add extra spices, as you wish. The meal is self serve. So first, you place, for example, a piece of fish from a serving dish, on top of your bowl of rice and then add herbs and chili. Then throughout the meal add more fish, herbs, and rice to your bowl.

A custom in the North is to serve others before yourself. If you are a guest at the table, expect your Vietnamese friends to take your rice bowl and fill it with rice. But it doesn't stop there. When you are eating with locals, they will take a piece of food and place it on top of your rice (using their own chopsticks) we hasten to add. It can be an annoying custom! They keep an eye on your bowl, which in itself can make you want to check your chopstick technique. Your hosts will keep on adding food, until with a wave of your hand, you indicate 'no thank you', and they will immediately stop feeding you!

It is manners not to eat directly off the serving dish with your chopsticks. Use the serving utensils. Put your choices into your bowl. Don't order a dish and 'keep the dish to yourself'. All dishes are ordered for the table, to be shared together during communal eating.

In this next section, you will find descriptions of street foods and discover places to eat authentic northern street food. We have included traditional recipes so you can cook your favorite street dishes when you get back home.

Miền Luồn
Eel vermicilli

Eel is very popular in Vietnam. Eels caught in the Red, Black and Song Ma Rivers, are firm fatty fish, rich in taste and flavor.

Our friend Quan invited us to eat eel with him in a restaurant at 87 Hang Dieu, Hoan Kiem District. This is a fishy place, in an excellent way. A place devoted to the eel! The first thing you notice is a mountain of eel stacked and packed in the entrance glass cabinet, bowls steaming with noodles and fresh crispy mung beans. Eel for breakfast, lunch and dinner. You've got to love it! We went upstairs, the ceiling stud was so low, sitting down on tiny chairs gave the feeling of being shrunk into a dollhouse. Quan ordered our meals for us because the menu was all in Vietnamese but recently the restaurant has been refurbished and posters on the walls show photographs of the dishes to make ordering food easier. Here is a sample of eel dishes on the extensive menu:

Lươn chả - grilled eel.
Lươn cháo - eel porridge; not a western style porridge, it's rice gruel with fried eel served with lettuce

and herbs.
Lươn khô - dried eel.
Lươn xào mỳ - fried eel and wheat noodles.
Lươn xào - deep fried eel.
Miến lươn nước - vermicelli with eel (broth).
Miến lươn tron - vermicelli and round eel, stir fried or in a soup.
Miến lươn xào - vermicelli and fried eel.
Súp lươn - delicious eel soup with vermicelli noodles and fried eel.
Miến tron - noodles tossed with eel, cucumber, and herbs.

Lu'o'n Nu'o'ng Xa
Eel chargrilled with lemongrass

Serves: 4-6

Ingredients
500g/1lb 2 oz eel fillets, boned, with skin on, cut into 5cm/ 2 inch pieces or use a firm fish, like mackerel.
1 small handful coriander (cilantro)

Marinade
1 tsp Thai red curry powder
1 tsp turmeric
2 lemongrass stems, white part only, finely chopped
2 garlic cloves, finely chopped
1 tsp sugar
2 tsp fish sauce
2 tbsp vegetable oil

Method
Combine all marinade ingredients together in a bowl. Add I tsp each of salt and freshly ground black pepper. Add eel and carrot. Mix together. Cover and set aside at room temperature in the marinade. Drain eel well.

Reserve Marinade
Heat barbeque grill of chargrill pan to medium. Cook the

eel for 3 minutes on each side. Brush with reserved marinade as it cooks. Remove and place in a serving bowl. Garnish with coriander. Serve with jasmine rice.

Lươn Om Nước Sốt Caramel
Eel braised with caramel sauce

Traditionally a Northern dish from the highlands, this dish is now found in different areas of Vietnam. The local name of this dish means 'three river eels'. If you can't find eel, use mackerel. The fat from this type of fish melts into the caramel sauce, making it delicious and velvety. Serve with rice noodles or steamed rice.

Ingredients
3 tbsp raw cane sugar or palm sugar
30 ml/2 tbsp soy sauce
45 ml/3 tbsp nuoc mam (fish sauce)
2 garlic cloves, crushed
2 dried red chilies
2-3 star anise
4-5 black peppercorns

350g/12oz eel on the bone, cut into 2.5cm/1in thick chunks
4 spring onions (scallions) cut into bite-size pieces
30ml/2tbsp sesame or vegetable oil
5cm/2in fresh root ginger, peeled and cut into matchsticks,
salt
chopped fresh coriander (cilantro) to garnish

Method

Put sugar in a heavy wok or pan with 30ml/2tbsp water. Gently heat until it turns golden. Remove pan from heat. Stir in soy sauce and nuoc mam with 120ml/4fl oz/1/2 cup water. Add garlic, chilies, star anise and peppercorns. Return to heat.

Add eel chunks and spring onion. Coat the fish well and season with salt. Reduce heat. Cover pan. Simmer 20 minutes to let eel braise in sauce and steam.

Meanwhile heat a small wok; tip in oil and stir-fry ginger until crisp and golden. Drain on paper towels. Arrange eel on a serving dish. Scatter crispy ginger and garnish with fresh coriander.

(Also delicious using pieces of chicken breast instead of fish).

Bún Thang
Chicken noodle soup

Bun Thang is a chicken broth with chicken, thin bun noodles, thinly sliced egg and thinly sliced pork (cha lua) garnished with hot chili, herbs, bean sprouts and lime. A true local specialty and is a popular dish served for breakfast, lunch or dinner. It is unlikely that you will find Bun Thang any place but the North.

Bún Thang Hà Nội

Serves: 4-6

Ingredients
2 liters/70 fl oz/8 cups chicken stock
2 tsp sugar
3 tbsp fish sauce
2 tsp garlic
100g boneless chicken breast
100g pork fillet, trimmed
250g /9 oz dried rice vermicelli noodles

2 eggs, lightly beaten
2 tbsp vegetable oil
2 tbsp sliced spring onion (scallion)
1 large handful coriander (cilantro) leaves
1 large handful mint leaves
1 large handful Vietnamese mint leaves
90g/1 cup bean sprouts
shrimp paste to taste (optional)
1 bird's eye chili, thinly sliced
fish sauce for dipping

Method

In a large saucepan, combine chicken stock, sugar, fish sauce, and garlic. Add salt to taste. Bring to boil over medium heat. Add chicken and pork. Reduce heat and simmer for 20 minutes. Remove chicken and pork. Cut into 1 cm/1/2 inch slices when cool. Reserve chicken stock.
Place rice vermicelli in boiling water. Cook 5 minutes. Turn off heat and leave in water for 5 minutes. Rinse under cold water. Drain. Set aside.
Heat a non-stick frying pan over low heat. Beat eggs with 1/2 tsp oil. Pour a quarter of this mixture into the pan to form a thin pancake. Cook for 1 minute. Turn over. Cook a further 30 seconds. Remove. Place on a chopping board. Repeat until there are 4 egg sheets in a stack. Roll all together into a tight roll. Slice thinly.
Divide vermicelli among serving bowls. Place egg strips, chicken and pork to cover the noodle. Pour hot stock over

to cover the noodles. Garnish with spring onions and coriander. Add a pinch of ground black pepper to each bowl. Serve with Thai mint, Vietnamese mint and bean sprouts on a plate, to add to the soup. For a more intense flavor stir in 1/4 teaspoon of shrimp paste to each bowl. Serve with a slice of chili and fish sauce for dipping.

Bún Bò Nam Bộ
Southern beef noodle soup

Bun Bo is a Northern specialty similar to the cooking style of the former imperial court in Hue. Spicy, sour, salty and sweet. A delicious dish of sautéed beef with rice noodles and salad of mixed with bean shoots, mint leaves, lettuce, perilla (fragrant serrated purple leaves), lemongrass, and peanuts, fried shallots on top. You just take your chopsticks and mix it together, coating the noodles well.

Try: the street stall opposite Hang Xia market Hanoi.
67 Hang Dieu Street, Old Quarter, Hanoi.
Beside Café 5 in Da Tuong Street, French Quarter (a mother and daughter run a stall every lunchtime, at the time of writing.)
If they are ever closed, you won't go hungry. Three of our favorite places are in the alley called Ngo Da Tuong. Go up the street and you will see a busy lunchroom place with all kinds of dishes (just point to what looks good and all the food is fresh and excellent, especially the fish soup, vege-

tables and pork spare ribs braised in caramel) Further up, our most favorite bun cha (barbecued pork patties) place, family run in an inside courtyard of a French villa, next to Café 7 Da Tuong (just before Lieu Thong Kiet intersection).

Bún Bò
Beef soup

Serves: 2

Ingredients
100g beef fillet, thinly sliced
5g coriander, chopped
50g mixed salad greens
100g rice noodles, cooked as per packet and drained
1 tsp vegetable oil
1 tsp freshly chopped garlic
2 tbsp beef stock or water
50g beansprouts
2 tsp sweet and sour sauce

Marinade
1 tsp vegetable oil
1 tsp finely chopped lemon grass

Garnish

1 tbsp crispy friend shallots
1 tbsp white sesame seeds
1 tbsp roasted peanuts

Method

Marinade the meat: oil it and coat with lemongrass. Leave for 15 minutes.

Prepare each serving bowl by adding herbs and salad and topping with rice noodles. Lightly oil a wok. Heat till almost smoking. Add meat and sauté until meat begins to caramelize. Add chopped garlic and cook taking care not to burn. Keeping heat high, deglaze the wok with beef stock or water, scraping the pan to release caramelized juices, creating a brown sauce. Throw in beansprouts, cover and cook for a minute. Add a little sweet and sour sauce. Spoon beef and beansprouts with their juices into bowls. Garnish with shallots, sesame seeds and peanuts.

Bún Với Rau Thơm
Vermicelli salad

Serves: 4

Ingredients

250g/9oz rice vermicelli
2 handfuls fresh bean sprouts
1 Lebanese cucumber, finely sliced
1 handful of mint leaves, torn
1 handful perilla leaves, torn
1 cup iceberg lettuce, sliced thinly
125 ml/4fl oz/1/2 cup dipping sauce
4 tbsp oil
4 tbsp fried red Asian shallots
4 tbsp lemongrass sliced and fried.
4 tbsp chopped roasted peanuts
1 green mango, peeled and thinly sliced
Thin slices chili and honey-cured dried beef

Bò Mật Ong Khỏi
Honey-cured beef

Serves: 4

Ingredients
450g/1lb beef sirloin
2 lemon grass stalks, trimmed and chopped
2 garlic cloves. Chopped
2 dried Serrano chilies, seeded and chopped
30-45ml/2-3 tbsp honey
15ml/1 tbsp nuoc mam
30ml/2 tbsp soy sauce

Method
Trim beef and cut it against the grain into thin rectangular slices, then set aside.
Using a mortar and pestle, grind lemon grass, garlic and chilies to a paste. Stir in the honey, nuoc mam and soy sauce. Put beef in a bowl, tip in the paste and rub it into the meat. Spread out the meat on a wire rack and place into the refrigerator, uncovered, for 2 days.
Cook the dried beef on a barbeque or under a conventional grill oven.

Nước Cham
Dipping sauce

Ingredients

3 tbsp fish sauce
3 tbsp rice vinegar
2 tbsp sugar
2 garlic cloves
1 chili
2 tbsp lime juice

Method

Combine fish sauce, rice vinegar, 125 ml/4 fl oz/1/2 cup water and sugar in a saucepan. Stir over medium heat. Cook just until boiling. Cool. Add finely chopped garlic, chili and lime juice.

Đậu Phộng Rang
Roasted peanuts

Ingredients
250g/9 oz raw shelled peanuts

Method
Stir-fry peanuts over medium heat until a soft brown color. Crush peanuts until coarsely ground. Keep in an airtight container for up to 2 weeks.

Hẹ Tây Chiên
Fried red Asian shallots

Ingredients
100g/3.5 oz red Asian shallots
500ml/2 cups vegetable oil

Method
Finely slice shallots and wash under cold water. Dry and set aside on kitchen paper until completely dry. Place oil in wok and heat oil until a cube of bread dropped in the oil browns in 15 seconds. Fry shallots in small batches. Drain on paper towels.
Keeps up to 2 days in an airtight container.

Method
Cook vermicelli as per instructions on the packet. Turn off heat and allow to stand for 5 minutes. Drain in a colander. Rinse under cold water. Set aside at room temperature covered with plastic wrap.
To make the salad, divide the bean sprouts evenly among for bowls. Add vermicelli to each bowl. Cut cucumber slices into thin matchsticks. Mix cucumber, perilla, mint, lettuce, green mango and place on top of the vermicelli. Dress with dipping sauce and garnish with fried shallots, lemongrass, peanuts and slivers of dried beef.

Bún Bò Hue
Beef noodle soup from Hue

Another version of the bun noodle, bun bo Hue is a regional dish, the original recipe originated from the ancient city of Hue in central Vietnam. Popular with Hanoians'. Not for the faint-hearted among us, you have to be game to try and be a meat lover. The dish has thick noodles, cooked pork knuckles (optional) oxtail, sliced pork in a sweet, sour, and spicy broth with the fresh flavor of chili and lemongrass. Fried puffed bread is served with this dish.

Try: 3 Quang Trung, Hoan Kiem District, Hanoi.
14a Tran Quay Cap, Van Mieu, Dong Da, Hanoi.
67 Hang Dieu Street, Hanoi.
17 Ly Thuong Kiet Street, Hanoi.

Bánh Cuốn
Fresh rice rolls

Bánh cuon is famous. One bite of the delicate gossamer thin and soft rice rolls and you'll know why. You'll find these fresh rice rolls served in street side restaurants and alleys. We often left our muesli breakfast at home and walked to a popular banh cuon stall nearby our house. We would open the old French gate to find ourselves inside the walled garden of a neighboring house in Ho Bo De. There, the woman of the house took pride in her award winning banh cuon. Using a traditional family recipe for the steamed rice flour crepes, she cooked them fresh, in minutes. The delicate batter poured out into a circle on the gridle, then rolled off the cooking pan with one chopstick, in a single practiced movement that elevated the preparation of the wafer thin rice pancake to a culinary art form. She placed onto the banh cuon, a mixture of minced pork and wood-ear mushrooms, while we watched and wrapped each piece into a perfectly shaped cylinder. She placed these on our plate before cutting them into bite-sized pieces. Expect your food to be snipped into pieces with scissors! Banh cuon is served with a side dish of warm nuoc nam, a clear broth flavored with fish sauce, sugar, a slice of sausage and thin slivers of raw carrots. Pickled vegetables, fresh shallots, buttercup lettuce, bean sprouts and fresh herbs such a Thai mint and coriander are served on the side. You just dip everything into the warm broth using chopsticks.

Try: 14 Hang Ga, Hoan Kiem, Hanoi.
72 Hang Bo, Hoan Keim, Hanoi, an old family house where the owners have served banh cuon for over 25 years. Also try their chicken filling with an egg cooked into it or barbequed pork.
66 To Hein Thanh, Hai Ba Trung, Hanoi. They specialize in Banh cuon Thanh Tri, steamed rice dough with a flavorful nuoc mam (fish sauce) with thick

slices of cha lua (pork bologna) and crispy fried shallots. Try their steamed rice flour pastries Banh duc, Banh gio and Banh xoai - a pastry filled with a sticky-sweet paste of ground white sesame and shredded coconut.
89 Ly Tu Trong, Q1, Ho Chi Minh City. They have been selling the southern version of Banh cuon for over 30 years.

Bánh Cuốn Nông
Steamed ravioli rolls

Serves: 12

Ingredients
125g rice flour
4 tbsp tapioca
1/4 tsp salt
Filling
4 tbsp vegetable oil
4 shallots, finely chopped.
10 Chinese mushrooms, stems removed. Reconstituted in water, drained and finely chopped
6 dried wood ear mushrooms, reconstituted in water, stems removed and finely chopped
225g cooked chicken

1/4 tsp sugar
1 tbsp fish sauce
ground black pepper

Accompaniments

Garnish: Fresh basil, mint, coriander
240ml Nuoc cham (dipping sauce)
40g crispy-fried shallots
8 tbsp dried shrimp, pulverized to a powder in food processor.

Method

In a mixing bowl, mix flour, tapioca and salt together. Slowly pour in 300ml water in a steady stream, mixing to a paste with no lumps. Pour in another 300ml water and set aside.

To make filling: place saucepan over a medium heat, add some oil. When hot, cook shallots until soft and tender. Add both kinds of mushrooms. Sauté until cooked, about 10 minutes. Add finely chopped chicken. Season with fish sauce, sugar and pepper. Cool in a bowl covered with cling film. Keep the film touching the mixture so it doesn't dry out.

To make the rice noodle crepes: Heat an oiled non-stick pan over medium heat. Pour a little batter into pan, swirling the pan to make sure batter covers the surface. Cook for 2 minutes. Flip thin crepe onto a well-oiled surface. Sprinkle a generous amount of filling, a couple of inches from the bottom edge horizontally across each crepe. Fold the crepe over the mixture and roll up into a cylinder shape, like a cigar. Repeat until you have 3 filled cylinders. Place on a plate and cut cylinders in half and each half in half again. Garnish with fired shallots and sprinkle with dried shrimp powder. Serve with nuoc cham as a dipping sauce with herbs added to it.

Nước Mắm
Fish sauce dip

Makes about 120 ml

Ingredients
1 tsp rice vinegar
3 tsp sugar
1 chili, finely chopped
2 garlic cloves, crushed
1 tbsp freshly squeezed lime juice
2 tbsp fish sauce

Method
Bring vinegar, sugar and 60ml water to a boil in a saucepan. Set aside to cool. Add chili, lime juice and garlic. Mix well and stir in fish sauce. Add some thin matchstick slivers of carrot to the dip.
Keeps well covered in the fridge. Can be used as a dipping sauce of salad dressing.

Bún Chả
Pork barbecued patties

Bun cha is a specialty of Hanoi. Street vendors introduced bun cha at the beginning of the 20th century: the smoky aroma of pork grilled over small charcoal burners, means lunch is served. One woman minds the barbeque, fanning the flames with a paper fan (or an old, even vintage electric room fan) cooking the meat. It's like a double barbecue: slices of belly pork, and pork patties. Barbecued pork is served in a warm broth made of fish sauce, rice vinegar and a little sugar. Deep-fried crab and mushroom spring rolls can be ordered on the side. Dip these into the broth. Pickled garlic and fresh red chili, salad and herbs, vermicelli noodles are served on the table. Add into the broth.

Try: 2 Au Trieu, Hanoi.
21 Nguyen Huu Huan Street, Hanoi Old Quarter.
1 Hang Manh Street, Hoan Kiem, Hanoi
Ngo Dong Xuan, Hoan Kiem, Hanoi.
47c Mai Hac De, adjacent To Dong Xuan Market, pork grilled in the same way since the 1950's. Pork patties are grilled in lot leaves.
23 Nguyen Bieu, Ba Dinh, Hanoi.
7 Da Tuong Street, French Quarter, Hanoi.

Bún Chả
Barbeque pork patties

Ingredients
1 tbsp fish sauce
2 garlic cloves, chopped
8 red Asian shallots, finely chopped
1 tsp caster sugar
300g pork belly
350g pork shoulder
1 egg
4 tbsp chopped garlic chives

Bun cha dipping sauce to serve

Nước Cham Bún Chả
Dipping broth

Ingredients
300g caster sugar
100ml fish sauce
100ml rice vinegar
100ml lime juice
1 long red chili, seeded and chopped
3 garlic cloves, chopped
60g carrot, thinly sliced
60g green kohlrabi, peeled and thinly sliced

Method

Combine sugar, fish sauce and vinegar in a small saucepan. Heat over low and stir until the sugar dissolves. Allow to cool before adding other ingredients.

600g rice vermicelli
150g bean sprouts
1 butter or stem lettuce, separated into leaves
1 large handful coriander sprigs
1 large handful perilla leaves

Method

To make marinade for barbecue pork: combine fish sauce, garlic, shallots and sugar. Remove the rind from the pork belly and cut into 2 cm thick slices. Cover with half the marinade and leave 2 hours in the fridge.
Process the pork shoulder in a food processor until finely minced. Transfer to a large bowl with the egg, chives and remaining marinade. Cover and refrigerate for two hours. Heat a barbeque or grill to medium-high heat. With damp fingers form the pork mince into 3cm patties. Barbeque the patties and pork belly slices for 3-5 minutes on each side or until charred lines appear.
To serve, divide the dipping broth between 6 small bowls. Add 3 patties and 4 pieces of barbequed pork to each, put the remaining pork on a platter. Arrange noodles, bean sprouts, lettuce leaves and herbs on a platter Dip noodles and salad ingredients into the dipping sauce before eating with the pork.

Mỳ Gà Tần
Chicken soup

My ga tan is one of those Hanoi's secrets worth discovering. Chicken soup, not like Mom cooked. This soup is kind of a cure-all, a revival soup that picks you up when you're feeling down. Known by locals for its medicinal properties. Ask any Vietnamese and they will swear by the soup's healing properties.

The basis of the broth is chicken. In Hanoi, there are three poultry options: chicken known as running chicken (free-range) or 'lazy chicken' (barn raised) sold by other vendors. My ga tan uses black chicken, as an ingredient. (A small chicken, the black-bone silky, does actually have black skin). Aromatic Chinese herbs are placed inside empty soda or beer cans. Then the chickens are stuffed with the cans. The chicken is placed over heat, allowing the meat to soak up the flavors while it simmers. Ramen noodles are then added to the chicken stew. This is a specialty soup only found at a few venues.

Try: 29 Tong Duy Tan in Hoan Kiem District, Hanoi.
50 Hàng Cân, Hoan Kiem, Hanoi.

Bún Mộc
Meatballs and noodle soup

This dish originated in Moc Village, which is now Hanoi's Thanh Xuan District. The North of Vietnam is a place of bun soups - bun rieu, bun bung, bun thang, bun moc, the list goes on. While the ingredients differ, the soups share common threads: noodles, whatever the thickness, from thin threads of vermicelli to fat noodles, these and simmering hot stock along with local ingredients, are what bun is all about.

In a bowl of bun moc, the noodles are thin vermicelli, pork balls mixed with wood-ear and shiitake mushrooms, served up in a deep flavored broth. Bite-sized pieces of gio (pickled bamboo shoots), plump shitakes, pork pate 'sausages', slices of roasted pigs trotter and shredded chicken are often served as garnish. The good thing about soups, you can try the 'things that float' and eat what appeals to your taste buds, which more often leaves you with an empty soup bowl.

Try: 57 Hang Luoc Street, Hoan Keim, Hanoi.
10 Bao Khanh, Hoan Kiem, Hanoi.

Bún Mộc Hà Nội

Hanoi pork balls and vermicelli soup

Serves: 4-6

Ingredients

3 dried wood-ear mushrooms (or shitake)
250g/9 oz dried rice vermicelli
250ml/9 fl oz/1 cup vegetable oil
2 liters/70 fl oz/8 cups chicken stock
3 tbsp fish sauce
2 tsp sugar
100g/3 1/2 oz pork terrine (gio song), sliced in batons, thinly sliced (purchase from an Asian butcher) or cooked pork sausage
100g/3 1/2 oz fried pork terrine (cha que), thinly sliced (purchase from an Asian food market or use slices of roasted pork)

To serve

2 tbsp sliced spring onion (scallion) green part only
3 tbsp fried red Asian shallots
1 tbsp garlic, finely chopped and lightly fried.
1 large handful coriander (cilantro) leaves
1 large handful mint leaves
1 large handful Vietnamese mint leaves
90g/1 cup bean sprouts

Vietnamese shrimp paste to taste (optional)
1 chili, thinly sliced
fish sauce for dipping

Method

Place mushrooms in a bowl. Cover with water and soak for 20 minutes. Drain. Slice thinly. Place rice vermicelli in a saucepan of boiling water. Cook 5 minutes and turn off heat. Set aside for 5 minutes. Drain noodles. Rinse under cold water. Set aside.

In a large bowl combine pork paste and mushrooms. Knead well. Divide mixture in two. Set aside.

Heat oil over medium heat. Form half the pork paste into small balls using oiled hands. Drop into oil. Fry 2 minutes until golden brown. Remove from pan with slotted spoon. Drain on kitchen towels. Set aside.

Bring chicken stock to the boil in a large saucepan. Add fish sauce, sugar, salt and black pepper to taste. Reduce heat to a simmer. Shape remaining pork paste into small balls and drop into simmering stock. Remove with slotted spoon when they rise to the surface. Set aside.

Divide the vermicelli among serving bowls. On top of the vermicelli place equal amounts of fried pork terrine, and fried and poached pork balls. Pour stock over to cover all the ingredients. Top with some garlic, spring onions, fried shallots and coriander. Serve a separate platter with fresh Vietnamese mint and bean sprouts, to add to the soup. For a more intense flavor add about 1/4 teaspoon of shrimp paste to each bowl, stirring to dissolve the paste. Serve with a small bowl of sliced chili and fish sauce for dipping.

For a healthy version of this soup omit port terrine and pate and add thinly sliced roasted pork to the soup instead.

Bánh Ghoi
Pillow-shaped pastry

Filled with minced pork and wood ear mushrooms, with soft vermicelli noodles. These are deep fried and served along with salad and herbs and a dipping broth. Other deep fried foods are nem cua be (crab spring rolls), banh ran thit (glutinous rice balls filled with pork), and banh ran ngot (delicious but sweet, glutinous rice balls filled with sweet paste).

Try Banh ghoi at 52 P Ly Quoc Su near St Joseph's Cathedral, a friendly family run business right next to an old pagoda. Two massive vats of frying oil, tables inside and out front. Popular with tourists and locals. Plenty of coffee places around for after's and directly across the road, a shop selling traditional dried and glace fruits. Do just check on the preservatives/methods in the fruits before you purchase a tempting quantity.

Try: 52 Ly Quoc Su, Hoan Kiem, Hanoi.

Chao
Rice gruel

This creamy rice porridge is similar to a Chinese congee because the origins of the dish are from China. Popular with locals since the 1980's. A steaming bowl of hot chao makes a winter comfort food. Served with crisp fried pieces of banh quay, as breakfast or a late night snack. The broth, the rice porridge is cooked in determines the flavor. Variations are chicken - chao ga, pork - chao long, heart - chao tim, tripe - chao suon.

Try Chao at 20B Tran Xuan Soan, Hai Ba Trung, Hanoi.

Cháo Gao
Clam gruel

Made with clam meat, the porridge is rich in flavor. Served with laksa leaf (rau ram) onion, dried red chili and quay (fried bread sticks).
Chao is a creamy gruel topped with roasted peanuts, spiced dried beef and green papaya. Vendors sell chao from lunch to late afternoon,

Try: 214 Hang Bong Street, Hoan Kiem, Hanoi. The clams are raised in the

owners dam and served fresh every day. The rau ram (laska leaves) comes from Lang village. Open 10:30 am weekdays and 3pm weekends.
Corner of Ly Quoc Su and Ngo Huyen, Hoan Kiem, Hanoi.
9 Ngo Bach Mai, Hai Ba Trung, Hanoi.
26 Trân Xuân Soạn, Hai Ba Trung, Hanoi.
139 Pho Hue, Hanoi. You can have Chao with shredded crab leg here.

Bánh Đúc
Spicy gruel

In Hanoi, Banh Duc is a spicy rice gruel topped with minced pork and fresh coriander leaves or with fried and chopped peanuts, sesame seeds, salt, and lime juice mixed in. Served with condiments at the table: sweet pickled chili and garlic make a delicious addition along with a sprinkling of freshly ground black pepper.

Try: 46C, Pham Ngoc An Trach 1, Dong Da, Hanoi.

Cháo Ga
Chicken gruel

Serves: 4

Ingredients
1.5 liters of chicken stock or water
170g rice
85g sticky rice (or plain rice)
200g poached chicken, shredded
1/2 tsp salt or soy sauce
4 tbsp fish sauce
1 1/2 tsp finely chopped spring onion
1 tsp coriander
1/2 tsp pepper

Method
Put chicken stock (or water) in a saucepan and add both types of rice. Bring to boil and simmer. Stir to prevent rice sticking to the pan. Cook 1 hour (if mixture gets too thick add more stock or water. Add shredded chicken. Season to taste. Pour into serving bowls. Top with spring onions, coriander and black pepper.

Muc Nương
Barbecued dried squid

This is one of the most social snacks you will find on the streets of Vietnam, popular with locals and tourists alike. A chewy fish jerky treat served often accompanied with ice-cold beer or iced tea. The dried squid is grilled over hot coals, shredded and served with a red spicy dipping sauce and slices of a root vegetable that tastes like nashi pear and raw potato. The same vendor will sell pork pate wrapped in banana leaves. Banana leaves are unwrapped and the pate (like a long thin sausage) is skewered and grilled intil warm. Also served with the spicy red sauce.

Try: 36 Hang Bo Street, Hanoi.
Also to the right of St Joseph's Cathedral in Hanoi, an alley between two shops tables are set for breakfast with various stalls, and in the evening, the barbeques come out and muc nuong is cooked up.

Bun Rieu Cua
Crab soup

A crustacean flavored soup made from fresh-water rice-paddy crabs. One of the most vibrant colored noodle dishes in North Vietnam. Tomato, tamarind paste and annatto seeds give the dish its signature deep red color.

The soup is a crab broth with tomatoes, wine vinegar and black pepper from Pho Quoc Island. A medium sized bowl of broth comes with rice noodles; tofu, crabmeat and sometimes thin slices of beef. The dish is topped with fresh crab paste. Additional ingredients can be beef, fried tofu, and pickled bamboo shoots, depending on the vendor's secret recipe. A plate of fresh salad: sliced banana flowers, lettuce leaves, bean sprouts and herbs is served with the soup. You just help yourself to salad and condiments to taste, along with optional puffy fried bread sticks to dip in to the broth. The rice sticks can tend to be a slightly greasy, but tasty!

Another version of the soup uses banh da, flat green tea noodles, from Hai Phong, a city on the Northern Coast.

Try: 40 Hang Tre, Hanoi.
25A Bat Dan, Hanoi.
11 Dong Xuan, Hoan Kiem, Hanoi.
11 Hang Bac Street, Hanoi.
Thuy Khue Street, Hanoi. Go under the yellow arch with Chinese calligraphy symbols.

Bun Rieu
Crab noodle soup

Ingredients
1 kg small soft-shell crabs (salt-water crabs, or use frozen crabmeat)
1/2 tsp salt
4 red Asian shallots
Vegetable oil for frying
2 tomatoes, core removed and cut into six wedges
600g rice vermicelli
4 spring onions, sliced

Accompaniments
1 small butter lettuce, sliced
1 handful coriander leaves
1 handful Vietnamese mint leaves
1 handful perilla leaves, sliced (optional)
fish sauce

Method
Thoroughly clean small soft shelled crabs, taking care to rinse away any sand and grit. Pull off and discard the shells. Remove any roe and set aside. Cut the crabs in half and place in a food processor or a mortar and pestle. Mince very fine. Pass crabs through a sieve to remove any large pieces of shell.

Bring 1 liter of water and salt to the boil. Reduce to simmer. Slowly add crab paste to the liquid and stir gently. When the crab is cooked it will float to the surface. Meanwhile heat a little oil in a frying pan to high. Cook the shallots for 5 minutes or until translucent, add roe and cook for 3 minutes. Add tomatoes and allow to soften. Add to the broth.

Divide the vermicelli and spring onions between 6 bowls. Return crab to broth, reheat for 3 minutes. Ladle the broth with the crab, shallots and tomato over the vermicelli. Combine the lettuce and herbs in a bowl and toss. Add to the soup along with more fish sauce if desired.

Bun Oc
Snail soup

Hanoi's classic comfort food. A rich, spicy tomato soup with a generous serve of oc (large fresh water snails) served along with salad, fresh herbs and rice noodles, bean curd and, puffs of fried rice breadsticks and fiery chili sauce.

Try: 13 Hoe Nhai in Ba Dinh District, Hanoi
11 Dong Xuan, Hanoi is famous for bun oc. The living room of the owners house doubles as a restaurant by day and family room at night.

Nem
Spring roll

Nem are crunchy fried spring rolls. A specialty of Hai Phong, a port city near to Hanoi is Nem cua be: a feathery light spring roll pastry filled with crab meat.

Our friend Mai Van Phan, the Peoples' Poet of Vietnam introduced us to his favorite, nem cua. Other nem versions have vegetables and minced pork

Gio cuon: fresh spring rolls. Fresh rice wrappers filled with herbs, salad leaves, thin slices of pork or prawn and coriander, then rolled into neat cylinders. For a spicy kick, dip the rice rolls into a small dish of fish sauce with a slice of red chili added.

Try: 1 Hang Manh, Hoan Keim District, Hanoi.
18 Phan Boi Chau, Hoan Kiem District, Hanoi.
58 Dao Duy Tu Street, Hanoi.
Look out for nem in the south where they are called Cha gio.

Xôi Xéo
Sticky rice

Xoi xeo is a Hanoi tradition, popular with the locals, most vendors sell out by 9am. Basket women place a serve of sticky rice in the middle of a banana leaf or newspaper for you to take away. Look for women with baskets beside them on street corners. It is normally warm as the sellers have cooked it at home in the early hours of the morning. Patience is needed while waiting to be served, because locals on their way to work, tend to push in first, in a hurry to be served. Which often left us thinking, it seems foreigners are to be served last, if at all, until we figured out you need to throw money down into the basket and then when the vendor sees your money, a few dong, you get served. Like most all street food, to get the street price, don't be duped into paying more because you are a foreigner. Watch money change hands between a local and the seller. Pay local prices. The more respect you have for your money, the more the locals respect you.

Xoi xeo is made from glutinous rice seasoned with turmeric. Yellow beans and fried shallots are added as a topping. The rice is kept warm in baskets and one vendor usually offers a selection of toppings, such as – crushed salted peanuts and sesame.

Our favorite sticky rice is Xio cuc. Made from the Vietnamese fruit of longevity. It will be the only orange rice in the baskets. The taste is like sweet citrus and absolutely delicious. It's available November to February. Try it with green banana for breakfast and a good Vietnamese coffee. If we could eat it everyday of the year, we would! Xio cuc sells out faster than any other xio in town. Sometimes it is covered up in the basket so you need to ask for it by name- sounds like 'soy gook. Also look out for young green rice, weighed out and wrapped in banana leaves to take away. Delicious with green bananas on the side as a snack. Sold by basket sellers in season, after the first harvest.

Try: 35b Nguyen Huu Hua Street, Hanoi.
Xoi Yen, 35 Nguyen Huu Huan, Hoan Kiem, Hanoi.
37 Bat Dan, Hoan Kiem, Hanoi.
42 A Ly Thuong Kiet, Hanoi for xio with a salty pork skin.

Xôi Xéo
Sticky rice

Ingredients
3 cups glutinous rice
1 tsp salt
Peanut and sesame

Method
Soak rice in cold water for 4–6 hours (or soak overnight) Drain and rinse under cold running water until water runs clear.

Sprinkle rice with salt and place in a steamer lined with muslin cloth. Cover and steam for 30 minutes. Remove lid and check rice is cooked (when rice is cooked, rice should be tender all the way through).

Serve immediately or cover with warm damp cloth to prevent rice from drying out and hardening.

Eat rice with your fingers, dipping in the crushed peanut and sesame.

Peanut and Sesame Dip

Ingredients
4 tbsp roasted unsalted peanuts
3 tbsp toasted sesame seeds
Pinch of castor sugar
2 or 3 tsp salt

Method
Pound the peanuts and sesame seeds to crumbs in a mortar or food processor. Stir through sugar and salt. Store in an airtight container.

Pho Bo
Beef soup

Pho is one of those Vietnamese words that sounds nothing like it looks. You can get close to the pronunciation by saying 'fur'. We have seen tourists saying Po or Fo and getting nothing. So say Fur and you've got a good chance of getting what you want, or just point. Of all the street food, pho is a quintessential Vietnamese dish, a taste of Vietnam in a bowl. In Hanoi, the simple and humble Pho Bo, beef soup, has a cult following. Hanoians also lay claim to the origins of this national signature dish.

The original recipes come from Nam Dinh Province, which is southwest of Hanoi, can be traced back to the Co family. The Nam Dinh village lays claim to the original pho recipe and have retained their secret ingredients and cooking methods.

At night, you can catch a glimmer of fire under simmering stockpots in the alleys. The secret of pho is the rich broth, the ingredients used and the length of time the broth is simmered. The best pho happens when the stock is simmered over a charcoal fire all night. If a place is popular with the locals, likely the turnover is good and the cooks will keep up their standards. With a bowl of steaming pho in front of you, copy the locals and add lime juice, bean sprouts, chili or fish sauce, sweet sour pickled garlic and fresh herbs.

Another variation is pho ga, chicken noodle soup. Our favorite version is goose soup with pickled bamboo shoots. Find this in the alley of 5 Da Tuong Street. The woman beside the bun cha vendor on the right makes a great soup, with big noodles. You can ask for the finer vermicelli and she will place it in a basket and lower it into the hot broth for a minute.

North Vietnam to South, you will be served up variations of pho: shredded chicken, braised brisket or thinly sliced raw beef (this gets cooked in the hot broth) but the basic ingredients are the same: a spicy rich beefy broth, rice noodles, and thin slices of beef, fresh bean sprouts, Thai basil, chili sauce, a squeeze of fresh lime, ground black pepper, salt and pickled garlic on the side.

Choose a pho stall like the Vietnamese locals do.

Busy with a high turnover, blue or red plastic tables and chairs pushed tightly together near a charcoal fire with its large stockpot steaming with broth. For street food, nothing gets more local than this.

Try: Pho Gia Truyen, 49 Bat Dan, Hoan Kiem, Hanoi.
Pho Thin, 13 Lo Duc, Hai Ba Trung, Hanoi.
5 Da Tuong street, Hoan Kiem, Hanoi.

Pho Bo
Rice noodle soup with beef

Ingredients
For the beef broth
40g/1 1/2 oz fresh root ginger, cut into 5 pieces
350g/12oz shallots, peeled and sliced
5 whole star anise
1/2 tsp fennel seeds
2 x 7.5 cm/3in cinnamon sticks
900g/2lb beef shin
1 kg/2lb 3oz beef marrowbones
2 sticks celery, sliced
2 carrots, peeled and sliced
2 onions, peeled and sliced
8 cloves
1 tsp black peppercorns

5 liters/8 pints/16fl oz water
1 tsp salt

For the Noodles
300g/10 1/2oz dried/1cm/1/2 in wide flat rice noodles
200g/7oz fillet steak
2 tsp fresh Thai sweet basil
2 tsp mint leaves
5 red bird's eye chilies, thinly sliced
2 limes, cut into wedges
8 spring onions, sliced
4 tbsp fish sauce
100g/3 1/2oz bean sprouts

Method
Place shallots and ginger on a chopping board and bash with a rolling pin.
Heat a large frying pan over high heat. Fry star anise, cinnamon sticks and fennel seeds for a few seconds until they release their aromas. Remove from pan. Set aside. Heat pan. Add 2 tsp of oil and add bruised ginger and shallots. Fry over medium heat for 8 minutes or until golden brown. Remove from heat and add to toasted spices. Place shin of beef, marrowbones, celery, onions, cloves, black peppercorns, roasted spices, ginger and shallots into a large saucepan. Pour water over. Bring to boil on medium heat. Skim off any scum as it rises to the surface, with a slotted spoon.

Turn down heat. Add salt. Cover with lid. Simmer broth on low heat for 3-5 hours.

Strain broth into a saucepan. Chill overnight. Remove fat from surface.

For the noodles

Bring a pan of water to boil. Add rice noodles. Remove pan, let noodles soak for 10 minutes or until aldente.

Drain noodles. Divide noodles into 4-6 portions and place in deep soup bowls.

Finely slice beef as thinly as possible and arrange on top of the noodles. Place basil, mint, coriander, red chilies and lime wedges into separate small bowls.

Add the white part of the spring onions and fish sauce to the hot broth.

Sprinkle the green part of the spring onions and the bean sprouts over the beef and noodles. Spoon hot beef stock over and serve with herbs and chilies. Each diner adds their own preferences.

Quick Pho

Ingredients
2 liters/8 cups Campbell's Real Stock Beef
2 thick slices fresh ginger
1 brown onion, sliced thinly
2 garlic cloves, sliced
4 star anise
2 cinnamon quills, lightly bruised
1 tbsp sugar
80ml/1/4 cup fish sauce
375g dried, flat rice noodles
400g beef eye fillet, very thinly sliced
80g/1 cup bean sprouts
2 red chilies, thinly sliced
1/3 cup each of fresh basil, mint, coriander leaves, Thai basil, to serve.

Method
Place stock and 500ml/2 cups water in a saucepan with ginger, garlic, star anise, cinnamon, sugar and fish sauce. Bring to boil. Reduce heat to low. Cover. Simmer 20 minutes. Strain. Discard solids. Return broth to pan. Cover with lid and return to the boil.

Prepare noodles according to instructions on the packet. Drain well. Place cooked noodles into warmed individual deep soup bowls. Top with thinly sliced beef fillet.

Pour hot broth over noodles and beef. Broth will cook the beef. Top with bean sprouts. Garnish with chili and fresh herbs.

Bánh Đa Trộn

Banh da tron is a bowl of fat noodles, with sausage, tiny crispy fried fish patties, firm tofu and crushed peanuts white sesame, accompanied with leafy salad greens and fresh herbs. If you prefer thin glass noodles you can point to them.

Around lunchtime, banh da truon is served by basket women from two baskets, which they carry from their homes, balancing them on a pole over their shoulders. In one basket is a prepared pot of broth, in the other, all the ingredients to make the dish. Be prepared to sit down on tiny, and we mean tiny, blue plastic stools, guaranteed to make you feel you are back in grade school, year one!

Try: Around the area of 42C Ly Thuong Kiet, Hanoi.

Bún Dọc Mùng
Pork and noodle soup

Expect a generous serve of double pork in this popular meat-lovers dish: thinly sliced pork and delicately flavored pork meatballs. Noodles are placed in the bowl, hot broth ladled over and topped with meat and fresh green herbs such as Vietnamese mint leaves.

Try: 63 Xa Dan, Dong Da, Hanoi.
18 Bat Dan, Hoan Kiem, Hanoi.
Phat Loc Street, Old Quarter, Hanoi.

Bánh Tôm
Prawn dumplings

Delicious small deep fried dumplings best described as savory shrimp donuts made from a sweet potato batter and prawns. On the side you have fish sauce and slices of green papaya. Banh tom was originally sold only around West Lake in Hanoi, then more family vendors moved into Hanoi and the dumplings became available in the city. But if you like tradition, you can still find banh tom sold around the lake, like the old days, from 2.30pm to 5pm.

Try: Ngo Dong Xuan, Hanoi.
55 Hang Bo in the Old Quarter, Hanoi.
West Lake at 25 Phu Tay Ho, Tây Hô, Hanoi. In West Lake where Banh Tom originated from, there are plenty to choose from.

Bánh Xèo Hanoi Style

    This subtle flavored turmeric crepe pancake originated in Saigon, but that didn't stop Hanoians' creating their own version, of course. The savory rice-flour pancake is cooked fresh on the griddle and filled with cooked prawns and bean sprouts, then folded in half.

    The table has an assortment of add-ons. Cut the crispy banh xeo into bite size pieces with scissors, and then place in rice paper. Add fresh salad leaves, fresh herbs, slices of cucumber, and a homemade chutney relish of sour mango or papaya, then roll up and dip into a vinegary, spiced dipping sauce. Nem lui, grilled pork sausages, can also be ordered for a spiced sausage addition to the roll-up. Remember, when in doubt, copy a local!

Try: 18 Phan Boi Chau, Hanoi.
25 Lo Su, Ly Thai To, Hanoi.

SNACKS

Hoa Quả Dầm
Fruit in a glass

Chunks of tropical fruit, like mangos, guava, pineapple with shaved ice, coconut cream or condensed milk. Perfect pick me up for those hot summer afternoons. Often we stop on the street corners and eat hoa qua dam.

Try: 15B To Tich, Hoan Kiem District, Hanoi.

Chè Đậu Đen
Sweet black bean drink

A slightly sweet pick me up drink, made from black mung beans, topped with threads of coconut and coconut milk.

Try: 16 Ngo Thi Nham, Hai Ba Trung, Hanoi.
4B Nguyen Quy Duc, Thanh Xuan, Hanoi.

Xoi Chè
Sticky rice topped with sweetened mung bean paste.

The basics of this drink, if you can call it a drink, (put it this way you will certainly need a spoon to drink it) is sweet rice and mung bean paste. Depending on the vendor it can come with coconut cream and ice. A welcome snack and sit down on the sizzling summer streets of Vietnam.

Try: If you're in Ho Chi Minh City try the speciality Xoi Che restaurant at 33 Din Tien Hoang, Quan Binh Thanh, Ho Chi Minh.
6 Ngo Thi Nham, Hoan Kiem, Hanoi.
93 Hang Bo , Hoan Kiem, Hanoi.

Chè Thập Cẩm

A sweet snack made with coconut cream, tapioca, mixed fruit and the finest crushed ice. Served in tall clear glasses with a seperate bowl of crushed ice to spoon in. Served ice-cold in summer, seriously thirst-quenching in the heat of summer,

Che thap cam, can include just two to six ingredients or more, depending on the region and family recipe: Lotus seeds, taro, sweet potato, tapioca pearls, fresh mango slices, lychee, mango, pineapple, papaya, custard apple, mini fruit jellies, and banh troi (sweet balls filled with mung bean paste) and freshly grated coconut; the list goes on depending on the season. The Hanoi version has 12 ingredients for the twelve months of the year. And if you are in Hue, be sure to dig into Che Hue style, with thirty-six different ingredients in a glass!

Try: In Hanoi our favorite is 72G, Trần Hang Đạo, Hoàn Kiếm, Hanoi. Perhaps the most famous che stall in Hanoi is 31 Dao Duy Tu, in the Old Quarter.
In Ho Chi Minh you'll find great che at the Intersection of Le Loi, Ham Nghi, Tran Hung Dao and Le Lai Street. Once you know what che looks like, keep an eye out on the streets in the mid afternoon.

Chè Khúc Bạch
Rainbow drink

Creamy panna cotta in lychee syrup, with slivered almonds.

Serves: 4

Ingredients
50g/2oz dried split mung beans, soaked for 4 hours and drained
50g 2 oz red beans, soaked for 4 hours and drained
25g/1oz/ 2tbsp sugar (grated palm sugar is best)
For the syrup
300ml/1/4 pint
1 1/4cups coconut milk
50g/1 oz/1/4 cup sugar
25g/1 oz tapioca pearls
Crushed ice, to serve
15g/1/2 oz jellied agar agar, soaked in warm water for 30 minutes and shredded into long strands to decorate, or use long shredded coconut.

Method
Place mung beans and azuki beans in two separate pans with 15g/1 tbsp/1/2 oz sugar each. Pour in enough water to cover. Stirring constantly, bring to boil. Reduce

heat and let both pans simmer for 15 minutes. Stir from time to time. Cook beans until tender but not mushy. Add more water to the pan if needed. Drain beans. Chill separately in the refrigerator.

In a heavy pan, bring coconut milk to boil. Reduce heat. Add sugar. Stir until dissolved. Add tapioca pearls. Simmer for 10 minutes until pearls become translucent. Leave to cool in the refrigerator. Divide beans among 4 tall glasses. Add a layer of crushed ice, then azuki beans and more ice. Pour coconut syrup over the top and decorate with strands of agar or shredded coconut. Serve immediately with straws and long spoons.

Chè Chuối
Banana in coconut milk

Banana stewed in coconut milk is served as a sweet snack using root vegetables like cassava, sweet potato, pumpkin, and taro.

Serves: 6

Ingredients
8 tbsp very small tapioca pearls
240ml coconut milk

225g sugar
4 large bananas
Crushed ice to serve (optional)
4 tbsp toasted sesame seeds
4 tbsp toasted chopped peanuts
4 tbsp shredded coconut

Method

Place tapioca pearls in a bowl. Cover with warm water. Soak 20 minutes until slightly translucent. Drain under cold running water and reserve.

In a saucepan combine coconut milk, sugar and 240ml water. Bring to boil over medium heat. Simmer 10 minutes.

Peel bananas and cut them into 5cm chunks. Add to the coconut mixture with tapioca pearls. Simmer over low heat for another 10 minutes until the pearls are cooked. Remove from heat.

Serve hot in individual serving bowls, or in a glass with crushed ice. Garnish with toasted sesame seeds, chopped peanuts and shredded coconut.

Cà Phê Trung
Egg coffee

The combination of creamy soft meringue-like foam and intense coffee makes a decadent drink!

Try: Cafe Giang, 39 Nguyen Huu Huan, Old Quarter, Hanoi. The café first whipped up this up during the 1940s.

Coffee shops are everywhere in Hanoi, but Trieu Viet Vuong is known as 'coffee street', and for good reason. In Hanoi's Hai Ba Trung District, there are more cafes packed together in one area of real estate, than any place else in Vietnam. It's a place to walk on foot to discover teashops and cafes. Trendy cafes run by young business entrepreneurs, many offer tastings, oriental cups and teapots, coffee makers, roasted beans and single origin tea leaves, beautifully packaged to make ideal gifts. Most of these family-run shops have been there for decades catering to Hanoians' and their national love of coffee and teas.

Try: Cafe Tho at 117 Trieu Viet Vuong, Hanoi. A friendly family run cafe serving coffee for over thirty years.

Hanoi-Barbecue

In the evening, follow the smoke and the mouthwatering smell of spiced meat and fish cooking over fires. Where there's smoke, you'll find barbeque grills on tabletops. Relax with friends, locals and fellow travelers over tra da (iced tea) or local and imported beers.

The poultry and meat are marinated in: ginger, soy sauce, garlic, chili, caramel water, fish sauce. Point to what you'd like and the vendors will bring your selection to your table, adjust the flame and then it's up to you to cook over the tabletop burners. Use chopsticks as your barbeque tools.

Hot pots are also available: order the raw ingredients individualy or all together, of fish, prawns, meat and vegetables and cook them in broth at your table.

Try: 66 Hang Bong Street, in the Old Quarter, Hanoi.
61 Quan Su, Hanoi, they have marinated sticky pork ribs, enoki mushrooms and okra on the menu.
80 Pho Duc Chinh, Ba Dinh Hanoi is a popular grill street. At night it gets crowded with locals and tourists.

Best Duck

Vit is the Vietnamese word for duck, a little more expensive than chicken. If you like duck then you're in luck: duck is salt-crusted grilled or fried and can be found all over Hanoi. Glistening lines of glazed orange colored duck can be seen hanging in restaurant windows and street vendor cabinets.

Try: Co Van Dinh, 9 Hong Ha, Hoan Kiem, Hanoi.
Ly Van Phoc Street & Ngo Gach Street, Hanoi.

Best Skewers

If you like grilled skewers you're in luck; so do the Vietnamese: marinated chicken, beef, squid, sausage, paddy snails, shitake mushrooms wrapped in bacon, eggplant, tofu, okra, the list goes on. Served with condiments, dipping sauces, salad and herbs and cold beer or tea.

Try: 66 Hang Bong, Hoan Keim, Hanoi.

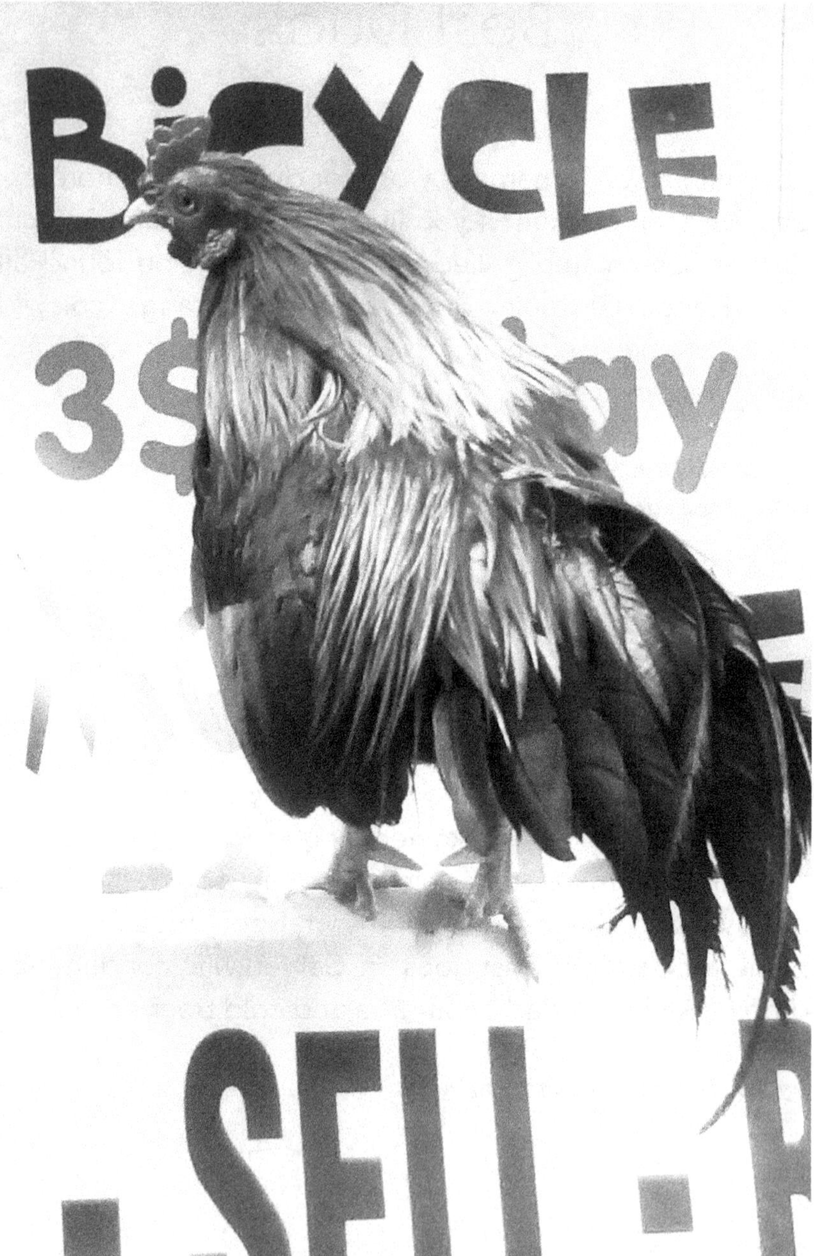
BiCYCLE

CENTRAL VIETNAM

Cao Lầu
Noodles and pork hot pot

Cao Lau is a dish only found in Hoi An. In Hoi An there are a number of variations, but the basic ingredients are usually a lemongrass broth to which is added: rice noodles and thinly sliced roast pork or shrimp. The garnish consists of fried bread croutons, butter crunch lettuce leaves, fresh Vietnamese mint, bean sprouts, chili and assorted condiments to taste.

Up to the 17th century; this town port was part of a trading route frequented by the Japanese. The main ingredients in cao lau are noodles rather like Japanese soba noodles. But unlike soba, they are made with rice instead of wheat and with water drawn from the city's ancient Cham wells. Hoi An has specialized Cao Lau restaraunts.

Try: Pho Cao Lau Hu Tieu, Stall 034, Hoi An Market, Hoi An.
6A Truong Minh Luong, Hoi An.
Thanh, 26 Thai Phien, Hoi An.
Lien, 26 Thai Phien, Hoi An.
Mi Quang, 117 Tran Cao Van, Hoi An.

Bánh
Steamed rice buns

One of the legacies of Emperor Tu Duc's reign in the imperial city of Hue is bánh. Steamed rice cakes eaten plain, dotted with chopped mushrooms, or stuffed with dried shrimp and served with a fish sauce. Add chili sauce to spice up these delicate cakes.

Try: Hang Me Me 16 Đ Vo Thi Sau, Hue, there is a large variety of different bánh on the menu.

Bánh Khọt
Hollow cake

Banh knot means 'hollow cake' made with rice flour, turmeric, mung beans and bean sprouts. The ground rice and coconut milk batter is poured into small molds to keep the center hollow for the filling; a single shrimp is added together with one mustard leaf, sea salt, fresh mint and Vietnamese basil. Served with a sweet rice vinegar sauce. Banh khot is eaten with herbs in a lettuce leaf. This dish comes from Vung Tau, a coastal town, 120 km southeast of Ho Chi Minh City.

In Danang and Hoi An, basket women sell Banh khot on the beaches. Also look out for small vendor stalls that sell ban khot at around 3pm.

Try: Banh Khot Ba Hai: 42 Trần Đông, 3, tp. Vũng Tàu.
Banh Khot Goc Vu Sua: 14 Nguyễn Truong Tộ, Vũng Tà.

Cơm Hến
Rice and seafood

Com hen is made with cooked rice, baby mussels or basket clams in a delicately flavored broth. In Hue you'll have fresh clams, from the Perfume River. Additional you can help yourself to crispy pork crackling, ground and roasted peanuts and toasted sesame seeds, fresh coriander, basil, Vietnamese mint and salad leaves.

Try:17 D Han Mac Tu, Hue.

Mì Quảng

Originating from the province of Quang Nam in central Vietnam. Mi quang is a must try dish, we really love this one. Excellent mi quang can be had on the street in Danang. In front of the Blue Sea Hotel at the beach there is a street where vendors sell mi quang for breakfast. Also the local beach market, (just off the beach) has a vendor who makes mi guang. You can sit inside the market, have mi quang cooked in front of you. The market 100 meters from the beach sells fresh fish and shellfish straight from the boats; which explains why the vendors ingredients: fish and crab cakes, shrimp, eggs and herbs always taste fresh, right down to the Phu Quoc island black pepper and fish sauce.

Mi Quang is made with thick turmeric noodles similar to fettuccine in size cooked in a rich fish stock sweetened with tomatoes, topped with anything from shrimp, pork and chicken, to fish, duck and even beef. Extras include hard-boiled quail egg and of course a dollop of chili and a dash of rich individualy created sauce.

Crispy deep fried banh trang cake is crumbled in and a spoonful of sweet-hot chili jam completes the complex dish.

Try: Mi Quang Que, 258 Dong Da, Danang City.

Bún Thịt Nướng

North Vietnam takes pride in its bun cha while locals in central Vietnam get fired up about bun thit nuong, their answer to bun cha. A simple dish that originated in Hue. Rice noodles, barbequed pork, local vegetables and spices all have a different flavor and piquance in the old capital Hue. Sitting down to bun in Hue is a chance to see how the locals do it in central Vietnam

Try: Huyen Anh, 51 Kim Long, Hue.

Bun Bo Hue

A home-cooked dish made with sautéed beef and drenched in a slightly spicy sweet and sour sauce, topped with fried garlic, spring onions and chopped salted peanuts. If you are going to Hue, expect the soup to be served with suon - pork rib.

Banh Khoai
Savory pancake

This popular savory pancake, similar to banh xeo, is known as banh khoai, famous in the imperial capital Hue. A crepe of generous proportions, made with rice flour, ground cooked short grain rice and coconut milk made from freshly grated coconut blended with water. The pancakes are cooked on a hot griddle when you order, then filled with minced pork meat, chicken or shellfish like prawns, Vietnamese mint and coriander, served with chao, a dipping sauce made from fermented soybeans.

Try: 2 Dien Bien Phu, Hue, has been run by the same family for more than three generations.

Banh Xeo Chay
Rice flour crepe

Crisp vegetable rice flour crepe with mushroom and tofu filling

Serves 6

Ingredients
100g/3 1/2 oz rice flour
25g/1 oz plain/all-purpose flour
1/2 tsp salt
1 tsp ground turmeric
150ml/95 fl oz coconut cream
150ml/5 fl oz cold soda water

Mushroom and tofu filing
50g/1 3/4 oz mung beans, soaked overnight until double in size
50g/1 3/4 oz store-bought deep-fried tofu
100g/3 1/2 oz oyster mushrooms
20g/3/4 oz dried shitake mushrooms, reconstituted, stems removed
100g/3 1/2 oz enoki mushrooms
1 tbsp vegetable oil
pinch salt and fine white pepper
1 spring onion/scallion, finely chopped

50g/1 3/4 oz bean sprouts
8 butter lettuce leaves
1 handful perilla leaves
1 handful mint leaves
100ml/3 oz dipping sauce

Dipping Sauce
55g/2 oz/1/4 cup castor sugar/superfine
185ml/6 fl oz/ 3/4 cup boiling water
3 tbsp lime juice
3 tbsp soy sauce

Method
Dissolve sugar in boiling water. Cool. Add lime juice and mix well.

Method
Sieve rice flour and plain flour together. Add salt and turmeric. Pour in coconut cream and soda water. Whisk to form a smooth batter. Rest 10 minutes before use.
Make mushroom filling. Steam mung beans until soft. Set aside. Finely slice the tofu and oyster and shitake mushrooms. Cut enoki mushrooms into 2cm/3/4 in long pieces. In a hot wok, heat oil and add mushrooms and tofu. Cook 2 minutes until browned but not cooked through. Season with salt and pepper. Drain in a colander and drain off any liquid.
To make crepe, heat a non-stick frying pan over medium heat. Sprinkle 1/2 spring onion in the pan. Pour one-third

of the batter into the middle of a 32 cm/12 1/2 in frying pan, cover the surface and pour remaining back into the batter (you want the crepe to be as thin as possible.) Scatter mung beans and cooked tofu and mushroom mixture, bean sprouts and remaining spring onions over half the crepe. Reduce heat and cook until the crepe is crisp and brown. Fold crepe in half. Slide onto a plate. Cut into 6-8 pieces. Roll up and dip into the sauce.

Banh Xeo Tom
Crepe with prawn and enoki mushroom filling

Serves: 6

Rice Flour Crepe
100g/3 1/2 oz rice flour
25g/1 oz plain/all-purpose flour
1/2 tsp salt
1 tsp ground turmeric
150ml/95 fl oz coconut cream
150ml/5 fl oz cold soda water

Filling
50g/1 3/4 oz dried mung beans, soaked overnight,

drained
2 tbsp vegetable oil
1 tsp. chopped garlic
400g/14 oz fresh prawns, shells removed, deveined, thinly sliced
200g/7 oz boneless pork belly, trimmed of fat, thinly sliced fat trimmed, thinly sliced
1 spring onion/scallion thinly sliced
50g/1 3/4 oz bean sprout
100g/3 1/2 oz enoki mushrooms, trimmed and cut into 2 cm/3/4 inch lengths.
pinch of salt and ground white pepper

Wrapping
12 butter lettuce leaves
1 handful perilla leaves' 1 handful mint leaves
100ml/3 1/2 fl oz fish dipping sauce (nuoc mam cham)

Method
Sieve rice flour and plain flour together. Add salt and turmeric. Pour in coconut cream and soda water. Whisk to a smooth batter. Rest 10 mins.

Prawn and Mushroom Filling.
Steam mung beans until soft, about 15 minutes. Set aside. Finely slice the prawns. Cut enoki mushrooms into 2cm/3/4 in long pieces. In a hot wok, heat oil and add garlic and pork belly. Cook two minutes. Add mushrooms and prawns. Cook 3 minutes until lightly browned. Sea-

son with salt and pepper. Drain in a colander and drain off any liquid. To make crepe, heat a non-stick frying pan over medium heat. Sprinkle 1/2 spring onion in the pan. Pour one-third of the batter into the middle of a 32 cm/12 1/2 inch frying pan, cover the surface and pour remaining back into the batter (you want the crepe to be as thin as possible.) Scatter mung beans and prawn and mushroom mixture, bean sprouts and remaining spring onions over half the crepe. Reduce heat and cook until the crepe is crisp and brown.

Using a spatula, fold the crepe in half. Slide onto a large plate. Cut into 6-8 pieces. Pick up a piece of perilla, mint leaves, place the crepe on the butter lettuce leave. Roll it up and dip in the sauce.

Bun Cha Ca
Fish cakes and rice noodles

Bun cha ca is a street food dish from central Vietnam. A delicate sweet and sour broth with rice bun noodles, Italian tomatoes, fresh slices of pineapple, fish cakes and bean sprouts.

Try: Bun Cha Ca Minh, Bach Dang, Nha Trang. They have been serving bun cha ca for over forty years.
In Danang try: 109 Nguyen Chi Thanh, Danang.

THE SOUTH

Xôi Bui Thi Xuan
Savory or sweet glutinous rice

Xoi bui thi xuan is a takeaway of fragrant sticky rice wrapped in banana leaves. Ben Thanh Market, in Ho Chi Minh city sells sweet and savory xoi thap cam or xoi ga (with chicken) with various condiments like salted peanuts, beans, coconut and shredded pork.

Try: 111 Bui Thi Xuan, District 1, Ho Chi Minh.
14 Truong Dinh, Q1, Ho Chi Minh City.

Cao Lầu Saigon

A Vietnamese version of the Japanese soba noodle in a lemongrass broth with additions of localy farmed shrimp, crab meat and roasted pork on the bone, fresh lime juice and savory sauce.

Try: Faifo, 139 Le Thi Hong Gam, Q1, Ho Chi Minh City.
Phu Huong, 21 Sao Mai, Tan Binh, Ho Chi Minh City.

Bánh Xèo Saigon
Savory pancakes

You can find banh xeo all over the country but this famous pancake has its origins in Saigon. The pancake mixture consists of a batter of rice flour, water and turmeric. Turmeric gives banh xeo its distinctive yellow color. Poured in thin circles, the batter cooks up light, lacy and crispy, like a French crepe. The pancake is cooked and filled with beansprouts, pork and shrimp, then folded in half. In Saigon the pancakes are known to be wafer thin and large in diameter, generously filled with minced pork and vegetables, they make a filling meal, rather than a snack.

Try: Banh Xeo 46A Dinh Cong Trang, District 1, Ho Chi Minh.
46A Dinh Cong Trang, Q1 Ho Chi Minh.

Bún Đậu Mắm Tôm
Shrimp tofu

Fried crispy tofu with mam tom (a fermented shrimp sauce from the north-central province of Thanh Hoa) gives the dish its pungent smell and to be honest, it's a smell that either drives you to the dish or away from it. We fit into the latter group! Pungent yes but if you are game, you can write and tell us why you and thousands of locals love this particular dish.

So let's imagine you are up to the challenge. The shrimp paste comes with sugar, salt and a little fat, you just add a squeeze of lime, sliced red chili, fresh coriander and Vietnamese mint and stir with your chopstick.

Also often eaten with cha com, which is thinly sliced pork sausage served with sticky glutinous rice.

Try: Co Khan, 102/1B Cong Quynh, Q1, Ho Chi Minh City.

Đậu Phụ Sốt Cà Chua
Fried tofu in tomato sauce

Serves: 4-6

Ingredients
500g firm tofu
Vegetable oil for deep frying
4 red Asian shallots, diced
4 tomatoes, skin and seeds removed,
1 chili, finely sliced
1 tbsp chopped garlic
1 tsp caster sugar
1 tbsp fish sauce
3 spring onions, sliced
Freshly ground black pepper
2 coriander (cilantro) sprigs to garnish

Method
Cut tofu into 4cm cubes. Pat with kitchen paper.
Heat oil in a wok or deep frying pan until a cube of bread dropped into the oil browns, approximately 15 seconds. Fry tofu in batches for 3-4 minutes until golden and crispy. Remove from pan. Drain on paper towels.
Heat 1 tbsp oil in a clean frying pan over medium heat. Add shallots, garlic and cook until translucent. Add tomatoes, chili, sugar and fish sauce. Simmer 10 minutes. Add

a 100ml/3 1/2 fl oz of water if sauce becomes too dry. It should coat the back of the spoon. Add fried tofu. Cover with sauce and simmer for no more than 1 minute. Garnish with spring onions and coriander. Serve immediately with black pepper as a condiment.

Tau Hu Xa Ot
Lemongrass crusted tofu

Serves: 4-6

Ingredients
450g/1lb) firm tofu
1 lemongrass stem, white part only, finely chopped
1 chili, finely chopped
1 tbsp. finely chopped garlic
1 tsp sugar
2 tablespoons vegetable oil
3 coriander/cilantro sprigs

Method
Drain tofu and slice into 5 x 10 cm/2 x 4 inch pieces, and then pat dry with paper towel. Leave the tofu on the chopping board. Combine lemongrass, chili, garlic, sugar, 1/4 tsp salt, 1/2 tsp freshly ground black pepper in a bowl.

Coat the tofu with the mixture. Heat a large frying pan over medium heat. Add oil and fry each side of the tofu for 3 minutes until the tofu is brown and crisp. Garnish with fresh coriander sprigs. Serve with jasmine rice.

Bún Bò Hue
Beef noodle soup

A southern home-cooked dish made of pork or beef, drenched in a slightly spicy sweet and sour sauce and topped with fried garlic, spring onions and chopped salted peanuts. The broth is rich and spicy, made from slow simmered stock bones. Fermented shrimp, slices of roasted pork or boiled beef, pork cakes and tiny crab cakes, float in the broth.

Try: Nam Gio, 189 Bui Vien, Q1, Ho Chi Minh City.

Bánh Mì
Bread roll

Vietnam's answer to the humble sandwich. A fresh French baguette, margarine or butter, a slice of homemade pork pate, thin slices of cheese, salami, pickled cucumber, cooked sausage, fried egg, cilantro and chili sauce. Makes a great breakfast when you take it to a nearby café and have with local coffee.

Try: Wherever you see bread rolls, hanging from roadside vendors stalls on wheels, with plates of fillings piled up inside the glass cabinet. Although not chilled and on first appearances, not super hygienic, the turnover is high and the food sells out fast.

Canh Bún

A tasty rice southern paddy crab soup with herbs and green fronds of morning glory, rice noodles, in the crab broth. Canh bun is rather like bun rieu (crab soup) except different noodles are used in the dish.

Try: 73 Ly Tu Trong, District 1, Ho Chi Minh.

Phở Bò
Beef soup

Pho bo tastes sweeter in the South: stir-fried lean beef cooked with tuong ngot, (sweet hoisin sauce), sliced spring onions, garlic and spices in a clear beef soup. Bean sprouts and fresh coriander, Thai basil, Vietnamese mint, and chili sauce, as accompaniments. If you're traveling the length of Vietnam it's a great dish to compare North to South.

Try: Pho Hoa, 260C Pasteur, Q1, Ho Chi Minh.
Pho Hoa, 323 Pham Ngu Lao, Q1, Ho Chi Minh.

Mỳ Quảng

Thick noodles, made with rice flour, sacred water and turmeric feature in this dish. My quang is one of our absolute favorites. And a must try dish if you are in the South. The cooked noodles are placed in a deep bowl and rather than a soup, an intense tasting sauce is ladled over. Served with deep fried banh trang (crispy cake) broken up into small pieces, and topped with any or all of the following: local cooked shrimp, roasted pork, poached chicken or duck, chunks of fish, and sometimes sliced beef. It all depends on the vendor's recipe and market ingredients. The dish is always topped with a spoonful of homemade sweet/spicy chili sauce. In each area up to the central coast Mi Quang has a distinctive difference of taste. Once you've done the distance you'll say oh my favorite Mi Quang is in... (where ever you had that 'oh yea' moment.)

Try: 21 Sao Mi, Tan Binh, Ho Chi Minh.
38B Dinh Tien Hoang, Q1, Ho Chi Minh.

Cơm Hến

This is a complex dish. Imagine the following ingredients in layers: clams fresh from the river, crispy pork crackling, ground roasted peanuts and sesame, fresh Thai basil, coriander and Vietnamese mint, thin slices of lotus root, thin green banana slices and slices of star fruit. Warm rice is placed on top and a spicy sauce poured over to make a fragrant, sweet and spicy with a little bit of crunch.

Try: Nam Gio, 136/15 Le Thanh Ton, Q1, Ho Chi Minh.
Tai Phu, 2 Dien Phu, Hue.

Bún Mọc

If you love pork, this dish is for you. Five different kinds of pork and thin vermicelli noodles, with a rich flavored broth all in one bowl. Cha lua: pork paste wrapped in banana leaves. Cha que: a pork paste fragrant with ground local cinnamon bark. Then moc (meatballs), three kinds: minced pork with wood-ear mushrooms, minced pork with shitake mushrooms and spring onions, and pork and minced garlic and fresh herbs. Garnished with: Gio (pickled bamboo shoots), shitake mushrooms, shredded chicken and slices of roasted pig trotter.

Try: 70 Ky Con Street, near Ben Thanh Market, Ho Chi Minh. Open 6am-9am: family run for over thirty years.

Gỏi Cuốn / Bì Cuốn
Freshly wrapped spring rolls

Fresh spring rolls originate from Saigon. The thin rice wrapper contains sliced boiled pork, shrimp, lettuce, vermicelli noodles and a green spring onion stalk. For bi cuon, shredded pork is used instead of rice noodles.

The spring roll debate goes on. Are nem in the North more delicious that cha gio in the South? Both dishes are different and it's just about preference. Fried spring rolls in the North are called nem ran: a thinner, flakier wrapping that's crisp on the outside.

The filling is generous and tasty. The fish dipping sauce is always hot and spicy. In the south, cha gio, is longer in shape, less greasy, the casing crisper, with more crunch to the bite. The fish dipping sauce nuoc cham has the sweet taste of palm sugar. You decide.

Try: 48 Ngo Duc Ke, Q1, Ho Chi Minh.
280 An Duong Vuong, Q5, Ho Chi Minh.

Bun Thit Nuong

South Vietnam raves about bun thit nuong. A simple dish that originated in Hue. Rice noodles, pork, local vegetables and spices. Bun or thinner rice vermicelli feature as a base ingredient in this dish.

Thit nuong ingredients are served up on a platter. Rice paper wrappers are filled with butter-crunch lettuce, fresh Vietnamese mint, Thai basil and cilantro, cold rice noodles and slices of grilled barbequed pork. Roll up (neatly) and dip in the sauce. Or sometimes the sauce is drizzled over and a tablespoon of chopped roasted peanuts and ground white sesame, added for garnish.

Try: Chi Thong, 195 Co Giang , Q1, Ho Chi Minh City.

Cháo

Chao is a rice porridge, usually made with broken rice grains; the texture is creamy, like a Chinese congee. Popular with locals since the 1980's. A steaming bowl of chao is winter comfort food. Served with crisp fried pieces of banh quay, (puffy fried rice bread) eaten for breakfast or as a late night snack.

Chao is served throughout Vietnam. If you are a poultry fan, watch for chao vit (with duck)

Try: Chao Ngoc Bich, 113 Pasteur, Q3, Ho Chi Minh.

Cơm Tấm
Broken rice and shredded pork

Com tam is the favorite of Saigon locals for breakfast and lunch. Follow the crowds and on most every street intersection, you will find com tam vendors. Com tam is the word for broken rice. This cheaper grade locally grown rice has the same taste Vietnamese rice is famous for, but the grains are not perfect, having been 'broken' during processing. Steamed, rather than boiled. Cheap rice means economical meals and perhaps why com tam has been popular since the 1930's. Served with suon (barbequed pork cooked with caramel water for sweetness) bi (pork shavings from a char grilled pig hock) and cha (pork cake with egg) along with options like chicken, fried egg, and thin slices of pickled cucumber, along with canh (a soup broth), served with the meal.

Try: 390 Cach Mang Thanh Tam, Q3, Ho Chi Minh.
Alley 150/7 Nguyen Trai, Q1, Ho Chi Minh.

Bún Mắm

This dish is all about seafood. Oceanic strong and intense flavors with vegetables, pickles, prawns, and squid in a sweetly scented seafood broth.

Try: 22 Phan Boi Chau, Q1, Ho Chi Minh.

Bánh Tằm Bì
Hand made noodles

Originating from Bac Lieu in the Mekong Delta. Although tam means 'silk worm' there are luckily no silkworms in the recipe. Tam are the short and thick handmade noodles. There are two versions, sweet and savory. As a dessert: coconut milk is poured over the noodles.

Another variation has barbequed pork with shredded pork skin added to the tam, garnished with thinly sliced carrots creating a crunchy topping.

Try: Banh Tam Bi To Chau, 27 Nguyen Trai, Q1, Ho Chi Minh.
Banh Tam Dong Thap, 352 Nguyen Trai, Q5, Ho Chi Minh.

Bánh Canh Trảng Bàng

This dish originally comes from Trang Bang, a town close to the Cambodian border. What began as a family recipe served to traders crossing the boarder, has become a popular dish in Southern Vietnam. The noodles are made with either tapioca or rice flour. The soup has variations depending on the family recipes: a popular version of the original dish is the crab-based broth, banh canh cua, with additions like cha ca, fish sausage and pork. The original banh canh uses lean pork and fresh herbs in a rich flavored pork broth.

In the Trang Bang District: from Moc Bai on the boarder to the Cao Dai Temple in Tay Ninh, you will see family run banh canh stalls.

Banh trang phoi suong is a variation where you make you own spring rolls at your table, by filling a rice wrapper with slices of pork, fresh basil, cilantro, Vietnamese mint, lettuce leaves and bo la lot; (beef grilled in lot leaves). Roll up your selection in rice paper and dip in homemade sauces.

Try: Banh Canh Hoang Ty, 70 Vo Van Tan, Q3, Ho Chi Minh.

Bánh Khọt

This dish comes from Vung Tau, a coastal town, 120 km southeast of Ho Chi Minh City. Like in Hoi An, Banh knot means 'hollow cake' of rice flour, turmeric, mung beans and bean sprouts. The batter is poured into small molds to keep the center hollow for the filling; a single southern shrimp is added together with one mustard leaf, sea salt, fresh mint and basil. Served with a sweet rice vinegar sauce.

In Vung Tau try: Banh Khot Ba Hai.
In Danang and Hoi An, basket women sell on the beaches.
Co Ba Vung Tau, 59 B Cao Thang, District 3, Ho Chi Minh.

Canh Bún
Crab soup

Canh bun is similar to bun rieu. Both dishes originate from Northern Vietnam. Canh bun in the south is a sweet and sour soup made with tamarind. The intense taste in both dishes comes from minced crabmeat and pink shrimp. The dish includes servings of spinach, tofu and pork sausage.

Try: 115/62 Le Van Sy, Phu Nhuan, Ho Chi Minh.
73 Ly Tu Trong, Q1, Ho Chi Minh.
491/20 Huynh Van Banh, Phu Nhuan, Ho Chi Minh.

Bột Chiên

A special rice flour batter, fried until crisp and golden with an egg cooked inside. Served with slices of green papaya, spring onions, chili sauce and rice vinegar pickles, as accompaniments.

Try: On the corner of Pham Ngu Lao and Cong Quynh, District 1, Ho Chi Minh.

Best Tabletop Grills

District 4's crowded street food strip in Ho Chi Minh City, is called 'the rustic quarter' by locals. Attracting locals with a menu of shrimp, octopus, calamari, chicken, pork, glazed pork spare ribs, okra and vegetables to grill at the tables.

Best Poultry

A café specializing in chicken: with marinated chicken legs and thighs over rice with spicy accompaniments is as popular as KFC in Vietnam. Although the cafe is always crowded, it has great atmosphere and real spicy tasting chicken.

Try: 288/6 Le Van Luong, Q7, Ho Chi Minh City. A garden setting 'Cay canh' in Vietnamese means 'tree and landscape': cherry, mountain apricot and small leaf variety of fiscus with twisted trunks and branches shaped into miniature bonsai trees.

Skewers in Ho Chi Minh

Smoky charcoal barbeques. Famous for marinated octopus, but if you don't like octopus, you won't go hungry. Choices include calamari, okra, pork marinated in caramel, glazed honey pork ribs, frogs legs French style, beef, buffalo and chicken marinated in fresh ginger and spices.

Try: Near the corner of Thao Thang 1, Tran Nao 1, Q2, Ho Chi Minh.

Bo La Lot Skewers

Seasoned ground beef wrapped in a peppery betel leaf and flame grilled over coals with dipping sauces. Makes a great snack with a glass of iced tea, iced lime or a local beer.

Try: 3T Quan Nuong, 29-31 Ton That Theip, District 1, Ho Chi Minh.

Sauces

The good thing about Vietnamese sauces is you can help yourself. All the condiment sauces are on the table, from chili sauce, to pickled garlic, to limes and salt and pepper. Help yourself and adjust the seasonings to taste.

One of our favorite sauces is the simplest: a little salt, a little pepper, a few slices of red or green chili, in a small china dish. You just squeeze in the lime and stir with chopsticks. A lime, chili, pepper, and salt dipping sauce that marries with traditional dishes, in a sublime way.

Ot Ngam Toi Sauce

Pickled chili in vinegar with whole or sliced garlic and a touch of sugar. Accompanies most soup dishes like pho and bun (noodles). Set on the table in a glass jar, help yourself. Raw garlic is thought to have healing properties. In fact, most of the spices and herbs in Vietnamese dishes have foundations in traditional medicine; from ginger to cilantro, garlic, chili, tumeric...the list goes on for ingredients that are 'good for health' according to Vietnamese tradition.Eating by the seasons means eating for health and longevity.

Tuong Ot Ha Noi Sauce

Hanoi's famous chili sauce. Less is more. Careful not to overdo it as this chili sauce can dominate your dish. Add slowly by the ¼ teaspoon and stir in. The sauce packs a pleasant aftertaste.

Ot Xay and Ot Bam Sauce

This is simply crushed and ground Vietnamese chili that goes with everything. From meat and fish to green mango and star fruit.

Ot Xao Sa Te Hoi An Sauce

Salty, vaguely oily. A hot sauce made with ground dried chili and fresh lemongrass. A specialty of Hoi An, served dry and you add the oil at the table.

Served with cao lau, mi quang, chicken and rice.

Ot Xao Sa Te Sai Gon Sauce

A Saigon specialty. A deceptively hot lemongrass sauce.

Tuong Ot Chai Sauce

A Vietnamese version of tomato ketchup. Basic chili sauce in a bottle. Mild, salty, and sweet. Served with French fries, fried noodles, fried rice and bo lac lac.

PHU

What happened to that crazy Phu Quoc dog? Sadly, we couldn't take her out of Vietnam because of strict quarantine regulations back in our home country. We left her behind with the couple whom we 'co-rescued' Phu, Bella, Beau and other neglected dogs from the streets during our respective tenures. Now today, on the eve of completing this book, we received great news about, Phu, the canine street food magician.

    Hi Sue and Bruce
    Hope all is well with you! I thought I would drop you a few lines to let you know Phu is doing great. She is a more difficult dog, than Beau (her father) in a few ways but is such a lovely character.
    The big news is we are moving to Arizona in early August. The dogs will be on the same flight with us in the hold- so it will be farewell Vietnam for Phu!
    I imagine they will love the Arizona heat:) Once we settle in, I will email some pics.
    Lots of love from us and Phu.
    Mark

This book is dedicated to all travelers who share a passion for traditional street foods of the world. Indulging in this unique slice of life, quietly supports the local people, culture and community. As long as the demand and interest in street food happen, the street fires will keep on burning and the soup pot keeps on simmering.

Enjoy your travels in Vietnam, North to South and take your fill of the most delicious traditional street food dishes available in Southeast Asia.

Best wishes from the two of us, the dedicated street foodies, Bruce and Sue

THE FAT NOODLE TRAVEL BOOK SERIES

500 VIETNAMESE STREET FOODS DISHES TRANSLATED FROM VIETNAMESE TO ENGLISH. FOR TRAVELLERS ON THE GO, WHO LOVE TO EAT ON THE STREETS OF VIETNAM.

NOW YOU CAN DISCOVER THE SECRETS OF THE HANOI OLD QUARTER AS YOU TRAVEL VIETNAM. 7 CAREFULLY PLANNED HANOI CITY WALKS, REVEALING VIETNAMESE CULTURE, HISTORY, LOCAL HAUNTS AND INSIDER TIPS, IN ONE TRAVEL GUIDEBOOK.

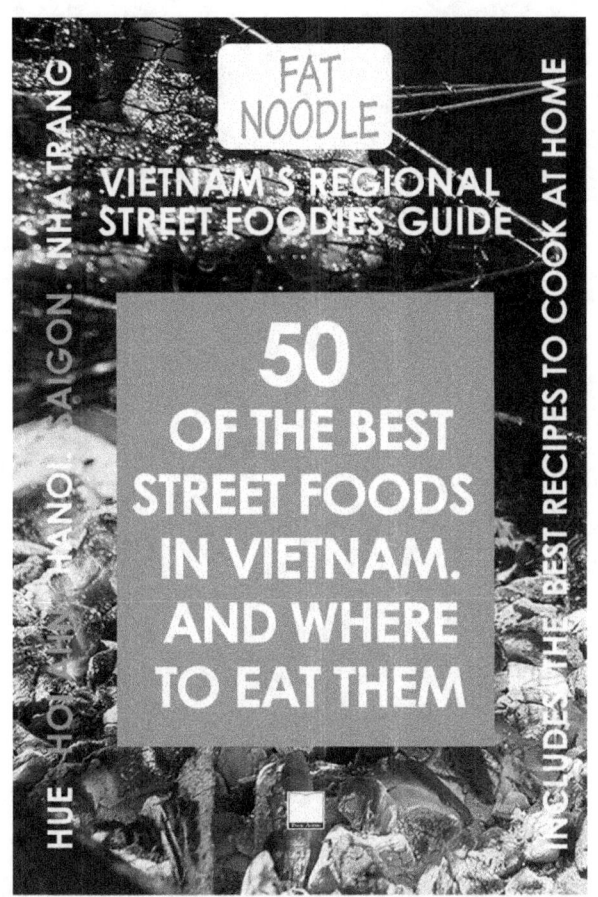

THE STREET FOODIES TRAVEL GUIDEBOOK TO REGIONAL VIETNAM'S STREET FOOD. INCLUDES FAMOUS STREET FOODS OF HANOI, HUE, DA-NANG, HOI AN, NA TRANG, VUNG TAU AND SAIGON. PLUS TRADITIONAL ORIGINAL VIETNAMESE RECIPES SHARED BY LOCAL VIETNAMESE COOKS.

www.ingramcontent.com/pod-product-compliance
Lightning Source LLC
Chambersburg PA
CBHW070627300426
44113CB00010B/1688